Metal Jam

Cathy Arnott

Metal Jam
The Story of a Diabetic

TERESA McLEAN

HODDER AND STOUGHTON
LONDON SYDNEY AUCKLAND TORONTO

British Library Cataloguing in Publication Data
McLean, Teresa
    Metal jam : the story of a diabetic.
    1. Diabetes   2. Diabetics
    I. Title
    616.4'62'0924   RC660

    ISBN 0 340 34744 9

Hodder and Stoughton Editorial Office: 47 Bedford Square, London WC1B 3DP.

Contents

Acknowledgments

Although primarily an autobiographical account of my life over the past twelve years, *Metal Jam* could not have been written without the help and co-operation of the following people and organisations. I would therefore like to thank them all, in no particular order, but with my heartfelt appreciation and gratitude:

Richard Cohen and Maria Rejt, my editors at Hodder, who together with Venetia Pollock helped so much in the shaping of the manuscript; Anthony Speaight and his pupil, for their advice on the legal aspects of diabetes; John Wilkins, for providing so much information on the history and occurrence of diabetes internationally; The International Diabetic Federation, for its generous response to my request for information; The British Diabetic Association, for its equally generous help, and the doctors and Diabetic Association officials worldwide, who gave so much of their time to answering my queries.

I would also like to thank Boots for their marvellous co-operation, and RHM Foods for giving so generously of their time and attention – especially Roy Drury and Brian Francis, who showed me round the RHM factory. Finally, I would like to thank all the doctors who have looked after me since 1973. I could not have written this account without their care, and suspect that in *Metal Jam* I do not thank them enough.

Teresa McLean,
January, 1985

7

Prologue

I am thirty-three years old and have been diabetic since the age of twenty-one. This book is about what it is like being diabetic and what it has done to me. It is a personal account, not a technical one, as I only know about diabetes from personal experience. I am nervous about writing it because I dislike the idea of writing about myself, but I am consoled by the hope that it might help other people who are diabetic or who live with a diabetic, if only because twelve years of exceptionally unstable diabetes have given me much more than they have taken away.

Many of the experiences I describe in *Metal Jam* are peculiar to me because, like every diabetic, I have individual symptoms as well as typical ones. The experiences I describe are in no sense typical or standard and I would hate to think that I might depress a newly diagnosed diabetic by recounting all sorts of traumas that are very unlikely to happen to him or her.

My opinions too are personal. They are not authoritative; indeed, they cannot be anything other than subjective, and I would not like to influence anyone's opinions of the medical institutions, personnel and treatment which I describe. I am writing impressionistically and if I offend anyone in the course of the book, I am profoundly apologetic. That is the last thing I would want to do.

Diabetes is not what I would call a first division illness; it is not like cancer or heart disease. It is not really an illness at all. It is a condition and one that never ceases to surprise and even sometimes entertain me. Diabetes is individualistic. It never affects two people the same way, and in my experience it never affects one person the same way for long. It is always changing. The only constant is its presence in my life, a presence which has given me opportunities and experiences I had not dreamt of; some terrible, some sad, some funny and some, unexpectedly, wonderful.

I have never had much sense of the future. It may or may not come. I wake up each morning amazed to find myself alive. I have always been like that. If I had had any conviction ten years ago that I would still be alive today, I might have planned what I was going to do, but I didn't. It is not that I thought I was about to die, but I thought I might be about to; you never know, and it seemed arrogant and, in some way I cannot explain, ungrateful to plan my future as if it belonged to me.

Perhaps because I had such a secure and happy childhood I sometimes used to daydream about myself as the victim of some tragic illness, bearing it heroically, admired by all. It was not quite as elevated as my other daydream of dying of a broken heart but it had the same romantic complexion. I imagined myself lying on a sofa looking tired but serene, smiling wanly at my visitors, who shook their heads as they gazed tearfully down at me.

Except possibly for the occasional bouts of tired serenity, diabetes is not like that at all. It is not tragic and it is utterly unromantic. Feeling ill with it is unlike anything I had imagined. I had a very romantic view of life; I still have, but not about illness any more.

1

Under the Apple Boughs

Now as I was young and easy under the apple boughs
About the lilting house and happy as the grass was green . . .
(Dylan Thomas, *Fern Hill*)

Everything about my childhood ran into superlatives. I was gloriously happy, a blessing I think I inherited from my mother, who has a simple enjoyment of being alive. My younger sister, Doe, was nowhere near as happy as I. We shared the same upbringing but while I remember playing garden games in the sun and indoor games when it rained, Doe remembers playing games she did not want to play and having snowballs put down her neck by our older brother, Anthony.

We were brought up in the house my parents still live in today, in a small village which is about thirty miles south of London. When my parents moved there after the war my father was the only commuter to London and my mother used to cycle round to meet him off the train. We lived next door to the one attractive eighteenth-century house in the area which was part of a German Catholic convent where I went to school.

The nuns had had a hard time of it when they came to England in the 1930s, after falling foul of the Nazis. When my father met them just after the war they were in dire straits. A Catholic and a lawyer, he felt sorry for them and helped them to acquire the elegant house next to ours. How he managed to get hold of it for them without any money I do not know, nor do I know how they managed to build it up into the sizeable community and school it is now.

The convent was part of my life. It surrounded our house; the junior school on one side, the senior school on the other. There was a walled garden, decayed and mysterious, with peach trees along the south wall and a water tank with a broken tap, full of brackish water. I remember an old barn which was always cold inside, even in summer, with garden tools laid out side by side in the dark and some wooden stairs up to the first floor, where apples were stored in autumn. The floor was 'unsafe' and I loved climbing up and lying there in the silence, smelling the apples.

They came from the convent orchard which stretched down to the railway line and was our favourite school playground in the summer. It was full of buttercups and at the far end, which was out of bounds, there were some bullocks and, some years, a donkey. The nuns took us into the orchard to make buttercup and daisy chains when it was too sunny to work, and to run around when we needed to 'let off steam', a condition they frequently diagnosed.

I always needed to let off steam and consequently seemed to spend a great deal of my first ten years racing about. There were two grass tennis courts near the orchard which were not kept up but were used for the sole purpose of running around. The lower court bordered on a big stagnant pond full of frogs and newts, and once, when we went there for a nature lesson, an otter emerged from nowhere. The pond was a dark place and also boasted an unsafe bit, like the barn: the boathouse, which was kept padlocked. Inside there was a rotten old rowing boat which we could see through cracks in the door. A huge oak tree overhung everything, plopping acorns down inaccessibly on to the boathouse roof.

12

Every summer the convent held a fête to raise money and we danced on the lower tennis court in front of our parents, dressed as Greek nymphs, piccaninnies, sailors, water sprites or whatever had taken our dancing teacher's fancy that term. I was not much good at dancing but I enjoyed it because we did it out of doors and I liked anything out of doors; the more energetic the better. I had all the usual childhood illnesses like measles and scarlet fever but was generally in what my father once described, to my vast amusement, as 'rude health'.

In the junior school we had drip-dry blue summer uniforms and when it was hot, the more dashing nuns used to turn the hose on us and we dried off by playing a sort of all-in rounders with hockey sticks and tennis balls. I liked sport. I still do and my favourite sport is still cricket, which I have loved ever since I can remember. The school had a great many West Indian boarders and we used to play cricket with them on the lower tennis court, where it was almost impossible for a good batsman to avoid hitting the ball into the pond. One fielder had to wear wellingtons to retrieve the ball, and both would emerge covered in slime.

We put a green oil drum on the grass, tucked up our skirts and played Caribbean cricket, the Trinidadian girls bowling fierce round-arm beamers, wearing brilliantly coloured skirts and gypsy ear-rings. The nuns thought it too dangerous to let us use a hard cricket ball so we used a tennis ball.

At home Anthony, Doe and I would play on the back lawn. We were out if we hit the ball into the vegetables, the rose briar or the French door without a bounce, and out if we hit it on to the roof. We developed techniques for hitting the ball into the mint, which gave us a chance to score runs while the fielders were looking for it, and off the house and garage walls on the rebound, which made it hard for the fielders to catch.

My brother came home from school one summer holiday

with a new cricket bat which we oiled lovingly with linseed oil, sitting on the back doorstep. I helped him break it in, tapping it gently for hours with a cricket ball, a proper hard one with a stitched seam. We never looked back. That summer Ant taught me how to spin the ball, we moved on to the field behind the garage to play and I learnt to bowl overarm.

I watched all the test matches on television and hung out of the trees for joy when my favourite batsmen did well. My brother had some old *Wisdens* and I loved reading them – loved just the look of them, with their ageing covers and their reverend, formal facts. Cricket is the only activity I know that makes statistics fun.

I played tennis at school and with my parents. School tennis was something of a mêlée because we only had two usable tennis courts between five hundred girls. We used to play twenty at a time, learning to aim straight so we did not get entangled in the next girl's strip. Family tennis, however, was a delight. We played on the convent courts in the evenings, my parents and my brother and I, with my poor sister mooning around, ball-boying.

The school hockey pitch was on a one-in-three slope covered with mole hills. I loved hockey and when I left school played in the village team, which was good uninhibited stuff, careless of class, weather and injury. I was a forward and liked it best on frosty days when we came in afterwards hot and exhausted.

Netball was more demure. It gave a certain deft satisfaction and I was glad to play in the school teams but I preferred hockey. Gym was well taught at school, with the accent on poise and control. The only athletic activities I was really good at were throwing things and long distance running. We went to the district sports and got laughed at by the other schools for being a convent and single sex.

I liked lessons, with the exception of science. The school had a dingy laboratory where we cut up dogfish and I punched holes in the tube of a Bunsen burner with my compass to see if it would gas me. I was not keen on maths either, but everything else I enjoyed. The nuns read us stories at the end of each day in the junior school and we got through everything from *Huckleberry Finn* to a volume of collected murder stories which we listened to with our heads down on our desks and our eyes shut. Once the sun came out during a French lesson after it had been raining and the whole class had to go out and look at a raindrop that was hanging off one of the bars on the climbing frame, because it was acting as a prism for the sunlight and refracting all the colours of the rainbow. A superb Frenchwoman taught us cooking and innumerable nuns instructed us in sewing and deportment, when we would have to balance books on our heads.

Until I was fourteen I was blissfully happy at the convent. Then everything changed when a new headmistress arrived. The old one had been tough and I had respected her. A German American who never smiled except in the teeth of disaster, she had an American faith in human nature and considered any admission of defeat 'flannel-footed'; any admission of impossible odds irrelevant. Her successor was a Canadian but seemed – to me anyway – without that inspired human quality. I thought her prosaic and took against her, particularly as she taught us religion in the sixth form, the one subject that I felt should not be prosaic but which I found increasingly dry, unmysterious and unreal.

I started to hate religion lessons. In a sense they had always been a penance because the few Catholics in school had to learn the Catechism while the non-Catholics read books and played rounders. I thought the Catechism was good but I would sooner have played rounders. Still, I liked religion and its trappings. The Corpus Christi processions through the gardens to the lower tennis court were a high point. The whole village came. We made an altar covered with flowers for benediction, collected petals and strewed them all along the way, then sang hymns and recited litanies, kneeling on the grass.

I liked that kind of thing but as I grew older I became impatient with the institutional aspects of Catholicism: details of Church offices and functionaries, Church politics, history and laws, without a grasp of the basis for them, left me cold. I did not mind curtsying to the bishop but I wanted to know the reason for bishops and the core of what they were supposed to represent. I became a bit of a fundamentalist. I thought we learnt too much adornment and not enough fundamental substance; too much Church and not enough God. I believed in God and wanted to try to find out why I did, but in an unintellectual convent like ours in the 1950s that was a recipe for disaster. The nuns quashed basic questions because they thought them subversive and I made trouble in religion lessons, annoyed that they could not see it was in a good cause.

By the time I reached the sixth form, which comprised only six girls, I had joined the Anarchist Society as a protest against enforced discipline, but found its monthly magazine disappointingly dependent on the structures and institutions that the society allegedly wanted to destroy. So I lapsed into school anarchy instead and began to study at home as much as possible. Lessons were inclined to be informal anyway, held subject to negotiation, sitting on the lawn, and I worked on my own more and more.

I had been trying to get myself removed from school for some time and had built up a record of childish crimes, ranging from setting off the fire alarm to planting a tree in the lavatory, where it took two nuns and two gardeners to get it out. My parting shot was putting the hose on Sister Monica, a quiet nun who taught domestic science, as she walked past our house. It was wicked. I made my sister turn on the tap so I could hose Sister Monica over the fence. I could not see over the top but I was rewarded with a shriek of horror I will remember all my life.

The trouble was, the exploit, once started, proved compulsive. Sister Monica could not stop shrieking and I could not stop hosing her. I just went on and on. In the end she made a run for it across a flowerbed, her head-dress all soggy and hanging off. I lay on the lawn and howled with laughter. I do not think I have ever laughed so much before or since. Within minutes the headmistress sent for Doe and me to come and apologise. We went up to the convent and there in the front doorway stood my victim, dripping, with an air of tragedy. The headmistress asked me if I was sorry and I looked at the puddle spreading round Sister Monica's feet and was overcome by the truth. I said, 'I know I ought to be sorry, Sister, but the fact is' – I could see my sister watching me anxiously – 'it was the best moment of my entire life,' at which Doe fled and I fell against the wall legless with laughter, beyond reach of human effort. It was more than time to be gone from school and I left, just after my seventeenth birthday, a little ahead of schedule. I still believed in God but disliked anything disciplinary about religion, such as compulsory attendance at mass because, in my time at the convent, I had never been given what I considered a convincing reason for it.

Still, a Christian understanding of life is the most important value my family and the nuns, despite our disagreements, gave me. I led a sheltered life and until I left school had no way of testing the line I was given on pain, suffering and death, which was simply that no one knows the reason for them, any more than they know the reason for happiness or indeed for existence itself. All one can hope is that they do have a purpose and once one believes that one can accept them, but trying to understand such mysteries is a trap, as the nuns never tired of telling me while I ground my teeth in frustration.

Offering your acceptance of everything that happens to you – good or bad – back to God, was one of the nuns' favourite themes. We used to pray to that effect every morning and it gave me the most delicious feeling of smugness to think that every small misery and injustice, like persecution by the nuns, could be turned to a good purpose if I wanted it to be.

After I left school, I did some short-term jobs but they soon bored me. I felt aimless and restless. There was nothing I really wanted to do, except possibly to write and I did not think seriously about that. If I had done, I might have learnt to type, joined a newspaper or done something helpful. As it was, I just indulged my love of music and wrote stories and poetry. Eventually my father said that he thought university would be a good idea so I took my 'A' levels from home and then my Oxford entrance papers, invigilated by a dozing nun. When I went for my interview, the principal of Lady Margaret Hall asked me why I had chosen to apply to that college and I answered truthfully that it was the only women's college I had heard of. I knew nothing about Oxford but I thought I might meet interesting people there. I imagined talking all night about poetry, watching cricket, learning obscurities from old dons, having traditional dinners in old colleges and being taken out by undergraduates reading English or possibly philosophy. I was incredibly naïve, had never been away from home for more than a few weeks and had no idea of what kind of work I would be asked to do.

Once I had been accepted by LMH, I indulged a whim that came into my head from nowhere and walked the Pilgrims' Way from Winchester to Canterbury, in glorious sunshine, taking ten days to do it. I worked locally, apple picking in the orchards, washing up in a hospital, working in a supermarket and, for a term, teaching at the convent, despite my villainous reputation there. I enjoyed it. I like teaching and over the years have gone back to it whenever anything else fails. I joined a voluntary work-camp and worked in a psychiatric hospital in Chester. There were about a dozen of us, all of roughly student age, from all over Europe. It was my first experience of communal living and the only one I have ever really enjoyed.

The staff resented us, coming on to the wards full of enthusiasm but knowing nothing. They gave us the most revolting work to do, like cleaning the lavatories, and the six of us who worked on the same ward developed a strong sense of solidarity, doing everything we were told with intractable compliance. It was grim work. We were assigned to the long term ward for male schizophrenics, most of whom had been there anything from twenty to fifty years and were institutionalised beyond all semblance of normality. When we had done our manual chores we were free to talk to the patients but mostly it was a lost cause. I had arrived with romantic ideas about madness being in part a kind of vision which saw things the rest of us could not see, but I was quickly disillusioned.

Indiscriminate eating was a hallmark of the ward. The curtains were bitten off up to mouth level; some of the patients ate their own faeces. It was humbling to work there and learn how little use I was, but there were moments of satisfaction too, which made it all worth while.

One day I took an old man, Mr Kennedy, out on to the field behind the ward to play croquet, having a vague idea that hitting things through hoops might be good for schizo-phrenics because it would give them an aim. We were not allowed to take patients out on our own and one of the tough, cynical, gum-chewing male nurses came with me and leaned against the wall while Mr Kennedy and I swiped at our croquet balls. Poor old Mr Kennedy was totally with-drawn. He never said anything and held his head rammed down between his shoulders, chin on chest. I got cold after five minutes and asked him if he wanted to go back in. But he clung to his mallet and refused to move, though he had only hit the ball about twice out of a hundred tries. He went on trying and I went on retrieving the ball and putting it in front of him. It started drizzling. The male nurse lit another cigarette and hunched his shoulders. We carried on. All at once Mr Kennedy hit the ball and it went through the hoop. He looked up and smiled. I shall never forget it. He whimpered with pleasure all the way along the corridor back to the ward. I decided on the spot to come back to Chester during my first Oxford vacation.

I did come back, on my own, every Christmas vacation while I was at Oxford. But the first time I went back I could not see Mr Kennedy. When I asked about him the nurses did not know who I meant. Then I showed them the bed he used to sleep in and they said, 'Oh him! He's dead.'

I was shattered. I had been brought up with a Catholic attitude to death, contemplating it last thing at night, praying for the dead, and going to boozy parties after funerals. I had been taken to see my first dead body when I was eight: dear old Sister Carpa, one of the German kitchen sisters, lay on a table with a chaplet of flowers on her head and a rosary in her hands. She looked sweet, as she always did, but as dead as a waxwork; she would never open her eyes no matter how long I looked at them. It was too awful to take in. I have always found death too awful and it was like that with Mr Kennedy, though his life was what most people would call a waste. He was old, frail and miserable but despite all that his death was heartbreaking.

Chester introduced me to the hard world I knew existed but had never before enounctered. Other than when visiting a friend with appendicitis I had never been in a hospital until I went there. I never went into one as a patient until I had diabetes. Hospitals were hushed places to be visited in the spirit you would visit a museum or an historic building, glad to come out into the sunshine afterwards.

But the time between school and Oxford had its enjoyable moments too. My parents' house stood directly opposite the village race-course and we were given free tickets to every race meeting because traditionally the villagers had a right of way across the course, and in return for not using it during a meeting one hundred local ratepayers were given free tickets. Most of the horse boxes arrived the night before the meeting and the stable lights were on late, with the horses neighing and sticking their heads out over the half doors. At dawn the next day stable lads in helmets and pullovers rode the course. By noon the car park was filling up and the television commentator parked his car in our field and had a drink with my parents.

My mother, sister and I went into the course by a back gate, each feeling very much one of the inside fraternity. The paddock was opposite the old convent house and we used to wave up at the nuns and boarders who hung out of the windows to watch. It was a pretty course and in those days in private ownership and attractively unkempt in parts. We watched the men in macintoshes whom you see at every meeting, whatever the weather, eating jellied eels (under a black umbrella with JELLIED EELS written on it) and spitting out the bones in a circle all round them. Old Raj Monolulu, who claimed to be some sort of a prince, and later wrote a book called *I Gotta Horse*, sat on a shooting stick, selling racing tips. He wore a Great War overcoat and a huge, tatty, multicoloured feather head-dress. His face was coffee-coloured and pock-marked and he used to give his customers a message written on a bit of paper, then catch them by the sleeve as they walked away and whisper something in their ear.

I like jumping better than flat races and went to every

jumps meeting, betting on every race. You could always find a bookie who was willing to believe you were eighteen when in fact you were twelve: my sister used to bet regularly when she was nine. I like backing outsiders, hoping for the big one against the odds. It only needed one success in a thousand tries to keep me at it.

My father never gambles. He is a safety first man, possibly because his father had gambled exuberantly and the family moved up and down Wimbledon Hill according to how the 'investments' had gone. One of my father's favourite sayings is, 'In the end it's the bookie who goes by in the Rolls.' I told that to the village bookie who was a doleful little man in a cardigan with a clapped-out Ford behind his shop. He gave a doleful little laugh.

My father is a profoundly, almost metaphysically, pessimistic man. He reckons it good going to get through a day without being killed, maimed, bereaved, bankrupted, cut off by the Gas and Electricity Boards, cheated, robbed, raped or run over; one or all of them. He believes in the ineptitude of life. Despite having almost nothing in common, we are very close. And I only found out when I went up to Oxford how much I relied on his presence and protection.

I arrived at Lady Margaret Hall in 1969, knowing nothing about Oxford: nothing about Evelyn Waugh's Brideshead Oxford or Newman's Oxford Movement Oxford; nothing about modern Oxford; nothing about Oxford traditions; nothing about degrees or careers. I did not even know what a tutorial was, or a punt.

I had never written an essay in my life. I had written 'compositions' at school: a day in the life of a penny; what I would do if I were a cloud; that kind of thing. I had written 'answers to questions' for 'A' level history, but not academic essays. To research and plan using primary sources of information was a new concept. So, being an innocent, I plunged into it all. I even enjoyed lectures, which no self-respecting sophisticate would have dreamt of attending, let alone enjoying.

But I did not find life easy. LMH did not have enough rooms for all its students and farmed the youngest of them out into lodgings. I was put in a convent lodging house, where I spent the first term feeling cheated; I had escaped the nuns at home only to be immured with nuns at Oxford. I also felt lonely. I found it harder than I had expected to make friends. The girls in the lodging house were kind but that was all. I joined societies and went to functions, but being the youngest and in many ways the most immature and inexperienced girl in LMH, I condemned most of the social life as pathetic.

Just once, I peeped in on the LMH tea party circuit. It was by mistake. I was asked to tea by one of the Roedean girls who made up the circuit who had somehow got the idea that I was circuit material. I sat and ate crumpets stuck on to the front of a gas fire with paper clips to toast. One of the party asked me something about Heathfield and I said I liked it. So did she, she said, and asked me when I was there.

'Oh, I've been there often,' I replied.

There was a suspicious pause.

'We are talking about the girls' public school, aren't we?' she said.

I told her I was talking about the point to point course, and was instantly expelled from the circuit, mercifully.

I worked hard in my little lodging house room and wondered where the magical, talked-about Oxford was and how one found it. At the end of my first term I decided it was not worth looking for and left. My parents were sympathetic but my father strongly advised me to return and insisted that Lady Margaret Hall move me into a room in college.

Life improved at once. I soon became very friendly with the girl in the room next door, started to meet people and to have a good time, though I was never completely happy at Oxford. The more I had a good time, the more I was afflicted with an uneasy feeling that it was all unreal, out of key with the rest of my life and the rest of the world. Reality soon became my other watchword – my first being enjoyment – and I could never quite reconcile the two.

Still, Oxford was good fun and for the most part I revelled in it; climbing in and out of colleges, learning about punts, Pimms and summer balls. I remember dancing on the tables at Magdalen wearing nothing but a shirt and going to night-clubs in London. I played a great deal of poker, I went to the races, to the country and to the theatre.

For the first time I encountered the world of money. I met an exceedingly rich undergraduate at Magdalen who took me to watch his horses racing. We drove down to Epsom in his sports car, which had a silver racehorse wearing his colours on the bonnet. We went into the paddock before the Derby to see his horse parade before running. We drank champagne like water and afterwards, at dinner in his London house, where I was waited on by a butler for the first time, he gave me a half-share in a racehorse.

The horse was trained by Scobie Breasley, one of Britain's foremost trainers, on the downs near Newbury, and I used to go and watch it train, without the faintest idea what I was supposed to be looking for, or where I thought it ought to run. Scobie decided all that. I just leaned admiringly against the stable walls. It never won a race so they sold it, after which it started to win. I didn't get any money from the sale because I hadn't paid anything towards the horse's up-keep. Mine was purely an honorary half-share but I was sorry to see it go, nevertheless – and furious when the horse started on a string of spontaneous victories.

As far as sport was concerned the going was good at Oxford. I gave up hockey because it could only be played seriously.

Instead I played tennis, swam in the rivers and one lucky day saw a notice advertising a women's cricket practice and went along. It was a wilted affair of torn nets, springless bats and old balls wielded by a few rather strong-looking girls. Women's cricket is a second class sport. Traditionalists consider it an act of vandalism against the poetry of the game, an aesthetic crime, but traditionalists once thought that about overarm bowling, which was probably invented by a woman. I play cricket for the simple reason that I like it. I do not expect or even want the same treatment as men cricketers. In fact I would almost prefer it to stay a second class sport because that makes it easier to excel in.

I bowled a few overs in the practice session and found, to my surprise, that I was better than the others, which was not saying much. I bowled, as the captain put it, deceptively; that is to say, no two balls the same. I bowled slow right-arm off breaks, but now and again a leg break and a googly by accident. The captain asked me if I would like to play in the team's next game. Of course I said yes.

We played a men's college and were annihilated, though they only produced a scratch team. All our best games were against scratch teams; when we played good teams who did not try, it was not much fun. We played two or three games against schools and they were the ones I liked best.

I remember one match in particular. It was a beautiful day, and we piled into a minibus and drove down lanes near Bicester, then up a long drive overhung with chestnuts and elms. We arrived at a Victorian house converted into a prep school. It was built in that gentle red brick which is more common in Berkshire and Buckinghamshire than Oxfordshire. The cricket field was in front of the house, encircled by elm trees. Small boys lay round the edges and watched, together with a few teachers and ladies in hats, sitting in deck-chairs. The boys beat us because they could bowl wrist spin, which we could neither bowl nor play. I was bowled by a Little Lord Fauntleroy figure, not much taller than the stumps, who nodded with crushing politeness as I walked off the field and said, 'Bad luck.'

We lay on the grass and talked to the staff, looking up at the sky through the trees. After the game the boys passed round trays of sherry in a dark, oak-panelled study. I have forgotten the name of the school. It probably does not exist any more and was doubtless never as lovely as I remember it. The elms will have died; it will have lost its charm. But that day it was perfect.

The university cricket season is ludicrously short, only eight weeks, ending with the varsity match in early June. I knew that people who played for Oxford or Cambridge got a blue but I did not know what a blue was, so I was thrilled to find a dark blue badge with a pair of crossed cricket bats and OUWCC woven into it shoved under my door the day before the match.

The varsity match was played on the municipal pitch along the Botley Road, as we were not allowed on any of the first class pitches and could not get a men's college to let us use one of theirs. The weather was bad and by the time we went in to bat it was pouring with rain, with intermittent crashes of thunder. One of our batsmen appealed against the lightning, but we carried on. I was nervous when I went out to bat at number seven, in torrential rain. I did quite well, because the fielders kept slipping in pursuit of the most pathetic strokes, but finally I slipped myself and was run out, after which the match was abandoned and called a draw. It might not have been the most scintillating cricket match in the history of the sport, but to me that didn't matter: I had, after all, gained my Oxford Blue.

Playing cricket was one of the greatest and most unexpected pleasures of being at Oxford, though the greatest of all was, of course, friends. I spent my second and third years inseparable from a man from Balliol called Martin, who was

26

one of the best dancers I have ever known. Martin and his friends were the hub of my life and everything else revolved around them. We wrote and read poetry, played tennis, had endless dinner parties. Martin spoke fifteen languages and I used to listen to him reciting poetry to the moon in Arabic, Chinese, Greek and whatever else came into his head. The day after my finals, Martin took me to the Derby, where between us we backed the first, second and third horses.

I enjoyed the work too, especially the last year of Byzantine history, which was exotically unfamiliar; I never got tired of trying to understand it. And it was because I did well in my Byzantine papers that I was viva'd for a first. A viva is an academic interview in which you have to defend what you wrote in the exams against the questions and attacks of a gang of dons. Mine was a fiasco. It was about a month after Finals; I had been on holiday and could not even remember what questions I had answered, let alone the content of what I had written. I just smiled and shrugged. 'Can't you say anything at all, so we can give you a first?' asked one very kind don, but I couldn't. I got an upper second.

When I left Oxford I had no idea what I wanted to do in the long term, though I did have one immediate ambition. I had been fascinated by India ever since I had seen some of Kipling's stories on television when I was about ten; now I wanted to see and experience the country for myself. At the age of fifteen I had discovered the poetry of Rabindranath Tagore when rummaging in a second-hand bookshop in Tunbridge Wells. It had confirmed my image of India as a romantic and spiritual immensity, but with enough cultural ties with Britain to make it accessible. At the same time I was aware of its poverty, or at least as aware as anyone who has not been there can be. I was not particularly socially conscientious and not at all interested in politics, but I was worried about poverty and misery and, equally, about my own distance from them. I had done odd bits of hospital and psychiatric visiting, and letter writing for Amnesty International but by the time I left Oxford I felt an almost desperate need to help people who had not had the plushy time I had been having.

I had never been outside Europe before and, by comparison, Martin and his friends were widely travelled, which made me feel underprivileged. So I wrote to Mother Teresa and asked if I could come out and help her in India. I had worked for her Sisters of Charity in London during one Oxford vacation and loved it. Nowadays there is a long queue of people like me wanting to work off their consciences with the Sisters but in 1972 all I had to do was write and they replied that they would have me.

Mother Teresa was then, as she is now, my ideal and I flew out to India the week after my viva at Oxford, full of excitement, awe and apprehension. The Sisters decided I would be most useful working at their place in Bombay and though I moved around a certain amount I spent most of my time there, teaching English and history. When I went out I was full of plans to work in the hardest jobs, but the first lesson I learnt from the Sisters was that everyone has a job that fits them, however undemanding and unimportant it may seem. I was more use teaching English and doing the occasional spot of hospice work than I would have been employed in a task that could be better done by Indians.

That was hard to accept but I was so overwhelmed by India and the scale of Indian poverty that I was often glad to get back from the streets and the dying children to the school, where there were chairs to sit on and cold drinks. The Sisters had no time for useless altruism. It was ironic that I went all that way, to a country with some of the worst urban poverty in the world, to learn that in the end I might be more useful to the world researching history at Oxford. For the Sisters believed that there was a divine meaning behind everything and that everything had a value, even if neither meaning nor value were apparent.

I was knocked over by what I saw in India and in all my time there was never able to sleep at night because of the wailing and sobbing in the streets below. It was years before I could integrate that experience with the rest of my life and then only intellectually. It was too much, too quickly, too separately.

I had gone to India with Martin, who had been there several times already and was staying with friends in Bombay. I used to rush over to visit them and pour out all my panic, horror and fear. He was understanding but the answers he offered struck me increasingly as hopeless. I think I must have caught a dose of Indian fatalism; that distrust of human effort which makes young Hindu mothers roll back their eyes and die without a fight. I could not believe that human effort would ever solve India's problems or, come to that, any of life's ultimate problems. I found Martin's talk about the need for education, American capital and international loans depressing; the more so as I was very fond of him and could not explain why everything he believed in suddenly seemed hollow. India tore us apart and he flew back to England, leaving me sadder than I had ever been in my life.

I felt hideously lonely. The Indian girls I worked with were charming and comforting, telling me that things were not as bad as I thought; I would get used to it. The Sisters were tough and kind. Their answer in the end always lay with God. But I stopped believing in God to any effect; I only believed in Him cerebrally and that was no comfort in the face of such urgent misery.

For the first time in my life I despaired. I walked along the harbour front, watching children picking over the rubbish heaps and grey, malignant Indian crows pecking at the beggars asleep on the ground, and wondered why I did not want to kill myself. Imperturbably, the Sisters said that they only

29

worried if people like me came to India and did not despair. They sent me to see a Spanish Jesuit who sat in a chair clad in pyjamas, fanning himself with a prayer book, and talked about need and faith.

I saw the priest each week for an hour and we seemed to discuss everything. He had a great effect on me, though I am not sure why. I think it was because of his indomitable personality. He justified his faith and because I believed in him I found myself believing in his faith too. I told him I thought I only believed in God because I needed to. He smiled and said, in his heavy Spanish accent. 'Of course. And whence comes this need? Hang on to this need as on to a rock in the sea. This you know is real. Soon you will know that what is behind it is real also.'

His faith made everything bearable, though it did not lessen the pain. It gave things an invisible, metaphysical and, in the last analysis, mysteriously hopeful context. Soon I found that my despair had mellowed into sadness. I started going to early morning mass with the Sisters. Every day I got up at five o'clock and slipped across from my hostel room to the convent, where an Indian priest celebrated mass each morning. Twelve years later I still think of those masses. They became reservoirs of strength and I understood why Mother Teresa says she could not keep going for a single day if she did not pray first. In the chapel we sat on a marble floor, the sisters, in their white habits with a blue line round the edge, curled into silent shapes, here and there a pair of brown feet sticking out. Mass was in English and we sang English hymns. Sometimes a bird or a huge, brilliant butterfly would fly in and dart about. After the last blessing we sat quietly for a few minutes, the fans going round slowly and the priest sitting on the floor with us in front of the altar.

Despite the soothing effect of the masses I found that I could only keep going physically with more and more of a struggle. At first I went for walks in the afternoon – like a mad dog or an Englishman – but I quickly gave that up and took a siesta like everyone else. I got so tired that I found it hard to wake up and harder to keep awake. I was getting diabetes but I did not know it, attributing my tiredness to the heat, the frightful humidity and the work, which had finally woken me up to what life was like for most people.

I became so thirsty that I drank the nearest liquid I could find: bottles of lemonade encrusted with ants, murky water, and endless cups of tea. I went to Goa for a few days' holiday and despite the boiling heat managed to get a sore throat which I could not shake off. Back in Bombay I lost my voice and had to stop teaching and working in the hospice. Surrounded by people so emaciated and so horribly ill, I was ashamed to admit that I felt below par. I carried on feebly, taking the antibiotics the doctors gave me but getting no better. I had got amoebic dysentery almost as soon as I arrived in India and over six months later I still had it. I felt too run down to go on, though I kept struggling along until I had to lean against the wall to stop myself falling over. In the end I was so weak the Sisters persuaded me it would be better if I went home. I agreed to go, feeling that I was leaving something unresolved.

It seemed a pity to return to England without seeing any of the countries on the way, so I went back overland. I made the long, oven-hot train ride across the northern plains from Bombay to Delhi, where I stayed with some friends of Martin. From there I flew up to Kashmir and stayed on a house-boat in Srinagar with an eccentric old Parsee lady, the friend of a friend of Martin. She did not really grasp who I was but made me welcome nevertheless, driving me round in her vintage car accompanied by an ancient servant, whose name sounded like Gaberdine. We walked through her pistachio orchards in the Himalyan foothills. I rode a pony up to the glacier line, floated across the Dal lake picking lotuses, ate Gaberdine's curries and scrambled eggs, and spent the rest of the time trying to avoid the Kashmiri army. They were on manoeuvres in Srinagar and made it hell for a woman. The locals pulled my hair and spat at me everywhere I went. It is a beautiful country but I was glad to leave. I was exhausted, wrung through a mangle. I was thin and hollow-eyed, my throat and chest hurt all the time; I coughed all night, drank all day and got on a coach to go back to Europe feeling like something from a Bombay rubbish tip.

At the same time I was sad. I had gone out there too young and was only just beginning, by the time I left, to cope with it all. For years afterwards I did not want to go back to India but now I would like to. It haunts me, the magic and the sorrow, and I miss it. I miss the excitement India gave at getting through a day alive. With life so cheap and so vulnerable, one could never take it for granted. India reduces, or lifts, one to essentials and it forced me to find what mine were in a hurry.

2

Tatters in Thin Trees

The spirit blows to tatters in thin trees
And whines and cannot reach the provinces.
(Peter Levi, *The stain is in my liver and my brains*)

During the time I was in India, my appearance changed so
dramatically that when my mother met me off the plane at
Gatwick airport she did not recognise me. I had gone out
there plump, and by the time I started back half a year later I
was so thin that the bones in my legs rubbed each other into
bruises whenever I lay down. I had lost over three stone in
six months and my face had become drawn and bony. I
rather liked it like that; it was more sophisticated, and I was
delighted to be thin.

The heat and the dysentery were enough to account for
some of it, but I later found out that rapid weight loss is one
of the most spectacular symptoms of diabetes. It occurs
because carbohydrates are not turned into energy. Instead
they lie around in the blood and clog it up in the form of
sugar, and the only way the system can get rid of it is to pee it
out. In India we ate an almost exclusively rice diet, and the
more I ate, the more often I peed and the thinner I got. I
could not understand it: ten times a day and three or four
times a night had to be abnormal, but I could only suppose it
was because I drank so much, and I drank so much because I

kept peeing it away. I was right in thinking that my raging thirst was caused by the loss of so much liquid, but I had no idea where the root cause lay. I just tried to make myself drink less, even when I was so thirsty that my throat throbbed; drinking three bottles of fizz in succession left me still feeling thirsty.

I think I may have been mildly diabetic as long as a year before I left Oxford because that is when I first started feeling thirsty all the time. I went on holiday to Spain with a friend and drove her mad wanting to stop for a drink every few minutes. We once got a lift from a charming Spaniard who thought this frequent stopping at cafés was part of being English, and happily kept ordering tea for us.

It was not always that bad. It went through phases, but when I got back from India I drank so much that my mother said there must be something wrong with me. She read out an article from a woman's magazine which listed symptoms of diabetes: weight loss, fatigue, thirst, excessive passing of water, dry skin and moodiness. 'You must be diabetic,' she said. We all agreed jokingly and did not give it a second thought.

My skin had got so dry over the past couple of years that it peeled off my feet and left them raw and scaly, with fissures that would not close up. My sister said my feet looked like bird's claws, and I smothered them with cream and kept them out of sight. I had changed emotionally too. I was certainly more moody than I used to be, mooching around and feeling sad much of the time. In retrospect, it is hard to believe that I could have been faced with such obvious symptoms of diabetes and not tumbled to it. But at the time it looked like a case of India sickness, and most of the symptoms had come on so slowly that, living with them every day as I had, it left me blind to their progress. I had always been so healthy that it never occurred to me that there could actually be something seriously wrong with me. And then there was always the spectre of all those Indians, so terribly thin and diseased, haunting my memory to stop me taking my puny problems too seriously.

But even with those excuses, I have to admit that I was slow on the uptake. I used to go to bed early, overcome by fatigue, and cry with frustration at having to get up and pee half an hour later. Except for six wonderful nights, each of which I treasure in my memory, I last slept through the night twelve years ago. I am used to it now and I have almost forgotten what it is like to feel rested. Almost, but not quite. On good nights I need only get up once, and feel a different person the next day. Then I remember how I used to feel.

It is hard to describe how enervating it was to get up six or seven times a night to pee. I was living in a bed-sit in London and used to lie in bed at night and pray for one, just one, night of unbroken sleep, then wake up to pee again. The bathroom was upstairs and I remember climbing up those stairs in the middle of the night, feeling the rush matting under my bare feet and looking out of the bathroom window at a white brick wall smudged with dirt. Going back to my room, I could hear the girl next door snoring blissfully.

I became nervous of going to plays or concerts in case I could not last until the interval without a pee. It was embarrassing to go out with someone attractive and keep disappearing into the ladies. I was delighted to be back in English social life and used to have lots of supper parties, cramming people into my tiny bed-sit until it looked like a scene from a Marx Brothers film, but invariably I was so tired by ten o'clock that I wanted them to go home.

It was more than tiredness, though. It was a weariness so profound that I used to wake up dreading each day; a draining, dismal lethargy that smothered any glimmer of enjoyment in life. All untreated diabetics suffer from this

35

kind of tiredness to some degree. It does not just come from broken nights, but also from having too much sugar in the blood – known medically by the Greek word for that condition, hyperglycaemia. In a normal body, carbohydrates are turned first into blood glucose then into energy, but in a diabetic the second conversion does not take place and the body therefore loses its main source of energy. Everything is an effort. Untreated, the tiredness deepens into coma, and if still untreated, death.

I knew nothing about that then, of course, and was simply mortified at feeling so tired. It was such a pathetic, nebulous complaint, like back-ache or nerves, and I told myself that this was what people meant by growing up; life could not always be exciting, and I tried to accept that and snap out of it. My mother says she remembers me coming home one weekend and lying on the floor and saying I wished I could go to sleep and never wake up. I had changed. I had lost my *joie de vivre* and become a millstone to my family and friends.

There was one friend in particular who disliked the new me. He was a magnificent Irishman who had turned up at home one day out of the blue, saying he thought he was a second cousin. Whatever his relationship to us, and I have never succeeded in working it out, Michael was a welcome addition to the family. He lived and drank insatiably, and took drastic action to try to cure me. He reckoned I should eat, drink, gamble and avoid the straight and narrow until I felt my old self again and began to do all that naturally. Michael was a kill or cure man, and I was lucky to survive his cure.

He had a friend who made poteen in a still under the Edgware Road and I drank a bottle of it, on prescription from Michael, every week. He could imagine no better complaint – nor one easier to deal with – than constant thirst, something he had suffered from himself for years. So we drank our way round all the Irish pubs in London seeking relief. Michael did not work. He seemed to be miraculously endowed with all that life required: a sports car in which he regularly had miraculous escapes from fatal crashes; a house in Kilburn such as only a single Irishman could bear to live in, with a chandelier and shirts covered with mould in the bath; enough time to be late for everything; and enough money to lose it habitually in casinos and never mention it.

A year before, I had to be dragged away from poker games with Michael at dawn, but that spring I did the unthinkable and declined a game one night because I was feeling tired. Michael was horrified. He had little time for the banalities of life, like jobs, fatigue and illness, and regarded my excuse as the death-knell of an ailing spirit. The secret of life was to be 'above it all' and I had somehow allowed myself to slip one notch below. I felt tired, when tiredness was all in the mind. Worse, I sometimes felt depressed when depression was an indulgence I would never have dreamt of allowing myself before I went to India. Like most people, myself included, Michael had put most of my being 'run down' down to India, so inevitably the more run down I became, the more he quickened the pace.

In spirit I was still game for anything, and the spirit was all that mattered in Michael's world. I could not even pretend I was physically ill – very much a second division excuse in his eyes anyway – because I had been in hospital straight after I got back from India and they had discharged me.

The first leg of the journey home had been a nightmare: the coach had broken down leaving us to hitch across Afghanistan and Iran, where I was robbed, followed, abused, spat on and attacked. Travelling alone, I made myself vulnerable to the best and worst in everyone I met. The best was fantastic, like the family who found me sitting on the steps of the Poste Restante in Tehran, too battered and exhausted to move, and took me in as one of them. I lived with these people for a fortnight and when I left, on the coach bound for Turkey, they lined up and cried. The father was a doctor and gave me some medicine to ease the dysentery for a few days and glucose syrup to build me up. It was the worst possible thing for diabetes, being concentrated liquid carbohydrate, but I drank it gratefully, broken-hearted to leave the family, who were a beacon of Muslim kindness and hospitality.

The worst side in people I met does not bear recollection but I blame myself for being naïve enough to travel alone as I did, inviting trouble. My experiences made me suspicious of everyone, especially people who offered me help, and I got into the habit of walking around with my eyes lowered, clutching my bag, ignoring people who spoke to me. By the time I reached Istanbul, I simply could not face any more of it. I was homesick, desperate to talk about everything that had happened to me, including the different person I had become. Being the only person who knew the new me was too much to handle, and I got a plane home.

At lunchtime I was in that other world and by suppertime I was in the kitchen at home, eating a cheese sandwich. My first cheese and my first western bread for six months. I had my first bath in six months, and lay wallowing for hours, feeling emotionally dislocated and too weak to get out. I also felt ill, though I told my mother – who thought I looked like something on loan from the morgue – that I was all right.

Wearing only Indian cotton clothes, I had slept out by the roadside crossing Afghanistan. The temperature had dropped sharply at night and I got the same sort of sore throat I had had in India, only this time my chest started hurting so much down one side that I could only breathe lightly. By the time I reached home it hurt down both sides and after my first night in England I woke up in agony, barely able to breathe. My mother called the doctor, who diagnosed pleurisy and called an ambulance.

I had never been in an ambulance before, and felt privileged as the ambulancemen bundled me up in blankets and carried me downstairs, joking about how nice it was to carry someone as light as a sparrow. One of them sat in the back with me on the drive to hospital and held my hand, saying we would not be long. I have had a lot to do with ambulances and ambulancemen since then, and familiarity has confirmed my impression that ambulancemen are without exception the nicest group of people in the world.

This was my first experience of hospital and not a bit as I had expected it to be: being wheeled in through the doors was like entering a luxury hotel. Thick carpeting covered the floor and there were huge, smooth lifts. The hospital was new and spacious, and I had a room of my own with a view of the town below; I felt spoilt, though the doctor later told me that I had to be isolated because of my lingering amoebic dysentery.

I lay back in bed and allowed myself not to care about anything. It was a relief to be cushioned from responsibility and from thinking about my future now that I was back home in England. I was too debilitated to think ahead and would have been happy to stay in hospital for a long time.

I was not allowed visitors and had to talk to my parents and Martin, who came, heroically, to welcome me back, through glass windows. I stood with my hands up against them, like a caged animal, and looked in misery at the roofs and smoking chimneys of the town outside. The very thought of going out into the ordinary world of cities and work made me feel weak; I could not envisage ever having the energy to face anything again.

They only wanted me in hospital for a few days. I took some medicine to combat the dysentery and had to attend out-patients for a few weeks afterwards. They gave me an injection of something – penicillin, I think – to get rid of the pleurisy and the pneumonia I had developed at the same time.

The doctor looking after me asked me if I had always been

that skinny; I said only since I had been to India. Then he asked me if I drank a lot, if I felt tired, if I had dry skin – I said yes to all three. He asked me to provide a specimen of urine and tests showed that it was full of sugar. All that was due to the dysentery, he said, and pinched some skin on the stomach between his fingers, showing me how it 'tented' – staying in the shape it had been pinched into. That was a sign of dehydration and is one of the tests doctors carry out if they suspect a patient has diabetes. High blood glucose draws water out of the blood by osmosis and causes dehydration. But this doctor ascribed all my troubles to dysentery.

How I missed realising I had diabetes, I do not know. How that doctor missed it, God only knows. When my condition was finally diagnosed, about four months later, I believe he got into trouble for his mistake. I hope not. But he did discharge me into the worst four months of my life, as far as health was concerned: I came out of hospital, on his instructions, feeling depressed and eroded.

Michael instantly pronounced that my spirit needed recharging, like a battery, and then all would be well. He helped me move into a bed-sit in London, and took me out in the evenings after work. I signed on with a temporary jobs agency, doing anything they found for me – clerking, cleaning, delivering – while I waited for the heavens to open and send down something to take hold of my life. The job I enjoyed most was working at St Joseph's Hospice, a home for the dying in East London. I have often gone back there since, working as an auxiliary nurse and domestic, and have invariably found it a boost to my spirits.

I had to get jobs that did not require sitting down because I had come back from India with a boil on my bottom which was so big and painful that I could only sit twisted sideways on one buttock. I had never had a boil before and have never had one since. Boils are a common sign of untreated diabetes

40

because germs thrive in sugary blood and cause infections which often erupt as boils.

I had got this particular infection on the journey back from India, and my main memory of the coach trip across Turkey is of lying prone on the seats, because it was too painful to lie on my back, as the coach jolted and skidded through the mountains by night. I was the only female on board and too shy to ask the driver to stop and let me out for a pee. I prayed in every village we came to that we would stop for the ritual drinking of *chai* (tea), and if we did not I curled up on one side and took my mind off my bladder by thinking about my bottom.

I could feel the boil but could not see it. It throbbed constantly and hurt if I touched it, and after one particularly dynamic bit of braking, which threw us out of our seats and crashed my poor bottom against the side of the coach, I let out a yelp. The man sitting next to me was a student and spoke a little English. He was polite and friendly all through the four days and nights on the coach, buying me *chai* at all the stops and warning me to keep clear of a little knot of bloodshot Turks in the back of the bus who were 'bad men'.

I came to look on Fareez (I don't know how it should be spelt but that is what it sounded like) as a protector; having him there was a wonderful relief. When he asked me what was wrong with my bottom – he had a beguilingly idiosyncratic and localised knowledge of English and pronounced it bot-hom – I told him I had a spot on it. We stopped in the middle of the night for the driver to have an hour's sleep, and Fareez took hold of my arm and led me about half a mile off the road into the fields.

'Please, I am going to do big work on your bot-hom.'

I was too tired to fight any more and could not help smiling.

'I bet,' I said and prepared myself mentally to be raped.

'Lie on front,' said Fareez.

I lay on my front.

'Remove bot-hom clothes' (pronounced cloth-ees).

I was wearing some sapphire-blue cotton *kurtas* – loose shirt and trousers – a tailor had made for me in India, and I undid the trouser cord and took them off.

'Much poison,' said Fareez, and I looked back over my shoulder to see him taking a knife out of his belt. All the Turks carried knives, and his was a curved dagger which he ran, hair-raisingly, between his lips. Then with one split-second swipe he lanced, or rather decapitated, the boil.

I could feel streams of stuff coming out of it. 'Much poison,' cried Fareez delightedly. 'Much poison bot-hom.' He produced a length of cloth which looked like an unravelled Turkish head-dress and mopped it up. I was overcome with gratitude and started to cry quietly into the grass.

'Please,' said Fareez, looking distressed and wiping my eyes with the other end of the cloth. 'Please.'

Afterwards he gave me the cloth to tie round my bottom, and I put my trousers on again over the top, looking like an overfilled suitcase. He walked me back to the coach, to a chorus of whistles and 'bad sayings' from the others, but before we reached it he stopped me and said unexpectedly shyly, 'Please, I wish to tell you . . .'

He looked at the ground and seemed lost for words. The coach horn sounded and we could hear the engine revving up. Then he came out with it all in a rush: 'Please, it is the first time I see a white bot-hom. I find it very nice.' This confession made me cry a bit more; if he had asked me to become his enslaved Muslim wife, I think I would have said yes.

The boil got less histrionic treatment at home. It filled up again when I left hospital and my mother said it needed a bread poultice. Michael, who was staying with us at the time and liked anything traditional, agreed enthusiastically. So I limped around with a scalding hot piece of bread stuck on to

42

my backside. I have to admit that the treatment worked; it drew lots of blood and pus, and the boil itself filled up and was poulticed half a dozen times in the next few weeks before finally dying.

Michael took me out for a drink to celebrate its death, at the White Hart in Fulham, where we listened to Irish music until the small hours of Monday morning. I was so tired at work the next day that I sat down for a coffee break and promptly fell asleep. I was working as a filing clerk in a hospital, which meant going down to the cellars full of medical records and collecting the files needed for that day's clinics, then wheeling them round in a trolley to their respective venues. The girl I was working with woke me angrily and said we could all skive off if we wanted but some of us had consciences. I was apologetic and worked extra hard for the rest of the day, darting into the cloakroom for a pee and a drink of water at every opportunity. That evening I lay down on the bed as soon as I got home and fell asleep fully clothed.

That night, before I went to sleep, I noticed that my ankles looked swollen. The swelling did not subside over the next few days and I showed it to my mother when I went home for the weekend. She said it was caused by too much walking around and told me to put my feet up. I lay on the couch with my ankles propped against the mantelpiece, grotesquely bloated. I put my finger into the swelling and when I took it out it left a hole.

I went to see my parents' G.P. in the village, but not because of my ankles. I went because I had stopped having periods. They had stopped once before, when I was seventeen – for no apparent reason – and I was delighted. It was only when I had been at Oxford for a year that I thought I had better go and see someone to make sure I was in working order. I saw the college nurse, who looked at me coldly and said, 'You're another one who wants to sleep with her boyfriend and be safe. Well, from that point of view I'd say you were laughing.'

I thanked her and left. There was no point in arguing. In any case, my periods came back for a while, before disappearing again. I did not give it much thought at first, but when almost two years had gone by, I went to my parents' G.P. because I knew he was a gentle, old fashioned sort of doctor and I wanted to ask him if it was all right to be like that. For although it had advantages, it made me feel as if I were not a proper woman.

The doctor was understanding and said it probably did not matter but just for my peace of mind he would get me an appointment with a specialist at the teaching hospital in London where he had been a student. Three weeks later I saw the specialist, who was business-like, trailing students in his wake. He examined me and said I was all right, though too thin.

'That is probably what has stopped you having periods. Go away and eat fattening things,' he said, ignoring my protests that I had stopped having them long before I had lost weight.

'Why are your ankles swollen?' he asked, just before he left.

I said I didn't know and he told me to try putting them up above my head and to come back in a year if I was still without my periods.*

I sat with my ankles on the window-ledge after work. I peed all day and all night, and consumed all kinds of sugary things with a suicidal obedience. I was so thirsty that I drank a bottle of squash a day, but refused invitations to go out for

---

*Irregular periods are common in diabetics. The connection between menstrual hormones and insulin, which is also a hormone – the one that is lacking in diabetics – is obscure, at least to the layman. But they are connected. Periods may affect diabetes, making blood sugar much higher, and diabetes may affect periods, making them more painful and unpredictable.

a drink because I was too tired. However, I staggered on for another two weeks, telling myself to pull myself together. One evening I got on a number sixteen bus back to my flat after work, and woke up when the conductor said we had reached the terminus. I had overshot my stop by miles. I waited for another number sixteen going back the way I had come, and this time managed to stay awake until the right stop, where I saw a plaque on a door advertising a group surgery and, for some reason I'll never know, went in.

I did not have an appointment; I was not registered with the practice and had no idea what my National Health number was. But one of the doctors saw me. She was an Italian, with a soft voice. She asked me what was wrong and, for lack of anything more obvious to say, I told her about my swollen ankles. She looked at them and stuck her finger into the flesh, which clung round the finger like glue.

'There might be something wrong with your kidneys,' she said, and told me to do a specimen of urine and bring it back the next day. I did one into a honey jar – the only container I could find – and took it round to the practice. She said she would send it away to be analysed, but just out of interest decided to test it for sugar there and then. She dipped a paper dipstick into it and the tip turned dark blue. She looked suspiciously at the honey jar, told me that I must have left some honey in it, and gave me a little bottle for a fresh specimen, which I was to bring back in twenty-four hours.

The next evening, the receptionist jumped up and told me to go straight in. I walked embarrassedly past the waiting surgery and gave the doctor the specimen, which again turned her dipstick dark blue.

'Do you pass a lot of water?' she asked.

I said I did.

'And feel tired?'

'Yes.'

'Sit there a minute and I'll write a letter for you.'

When she had finished she told me to take it round to one of the out-patients clinics at the Westminster Hospital as soon as possible. I said it would have to be the next week as I was working that week, but she shook her head and told me to cancel everything and take the letter round first thing in the morning. I was working as a receptionist in a group surgery near the Elephant and Castle, which was friendly and good fun and I was hoping to stay there as long as possible. They were sweet when I said I would have to miss half a day, and told me to hurry back.

I lived just round the corner from the Westminster Hospital and walked there the next morning. The receptionist in the clinic shook her head and told me I could not be seen without an appointment, doctor's letter or no doctor's letter. I turned to go. But she called me back, saying that she had better just have a look at the letter. When she had read it, she told me to sit down; she would see if the doctor could fit me in at the end of the clinic. I read recipes in women's magazines and looked around, feeling too tired and distanced to feel much else.

It was one-thirty before the doctor called my name. He was young and handsome in a stone cold sort of way. I apologised for making him late for lunch.

'It doesn't matter,' he said in broad Scottish. 'Take off your clothes and lie on the couch.'

He prodded and banged and listened, looking a long time at my feet and ankles, and into my eyes with a kind of gun-shaped light which I later learnt was called an ophthalmo-scope. He went through a litany of symptoms, from pins and needles to exhaustion, and I had to admit to having them all.

'Well,' he said. 'There's not much doubt in my mind that you're diabetic.'

I did not say anything because I did not feel anything, except a vague sense of relief that there was at last a genuine reason for feeling as low as I did.

'I think what we'll do is pop you in for a few days while we sort you out,' he said. I thanked him and asked if next week would be all right: he grinned his cold grin.

'My dear girl, I'm not letting you go upstairs to the ward on your own, never mind going out or to work. Go and sit in the waiting room for a minute while I get one of the nurses to look after you.'

I sat down meekly and shut my eyes; I was now officially licensed to feel tired. I fell asleep and woke up a couple of hours later to hear the same doctor shouting in his whiplash Scottish accent.

'Is that girl still here? For Christ's sake, I told you to get her upstairs and into bed. Can't you see how pale she is?'

I sat up, feeling important, and asked if I could go and get my night things from my bed-sit, as it was only a few hundred yards away. When my request was refused, I felt more important still.

'Diabetics in your condition can go over very quickly,' he said. 'Get into a chair and someone will take you up in the lift.'

I felt ridiculous being wheeled into the ward, which was a big one full of women moaning and snoring, and even worse when I was made to put on a white hospital nightie under a hideous, striped hospital dressing-gown.

I sat in bed and looked around. It was the dead time of the afternoon, and I lay against the pillows and wondered what diabetes was. The only diabetic I had ever come across was a man called Fred, who was the son of the convent gardener and used to come to the convent on Sundays to see his father. Inexplicably, he drove a Daimler, which had running boards and which he used to wash on Sunday afternoons. He was all smiles and the picture of health. I wondered if it was worth ringing my mother to tell her the news.

Then a young doctor in a white coat marched across the ward, introduced himself as the houseman and drew the curtains round my bed. He examined me meticulously and asked an even more exhaustive litany of symptom questions than the Scottish doctor. He was one of the new breed of doctor: young, clever, quick and clinical. I said yes to most of his questions but one or two I could not answer. He asked me if my sex drive was normal. I said I didn't know; what counted as normal? He said it was obviously not because I would know if it were. Dr James was a great one for black and white, and anything I could not answer exactly emerged from his questioning a dispiriting shade of grey.

He was interested in my ankles, and said that the swelling was called oedema. He also pushed a pencil into them to demonstrate that it was pitting oedema because any pressure created pits. The condition is caused by a deposit of excess water and normally results from heart or kidney disease, but in my case it was caused by water and sugar, an unusual by-product of diabetes. He gave me diuretics to take, which meant I got no relief from the constant peeing, but over the next few weeks my ankles, at least, went back to normal.

Dr James was also interested in my feet, which had turned pale mauve and lay skinny and scaly on the sheet, with cracks across them that oozed drops of blood when touched. He took a pin out of his lapel and told me to shut my eyes and tell him when I could feel him pricking my feet. I felt a few pricks but he said I had missed most of them.

'Why the hell didn't you come to us earlier?' he asked. 'When you've got to the stage of impaired feeling like this, you're in a bad way. You couldn't have gone on for much longer like this.'

He carried on shaking his head and took a big syringe off a little cardboard tray he had put on the bedside table, saying he was going to take some blood for testing.

I have never minded injections but I have always had a peculiar horror of drug addiction, which centres on the actual business of injecting. I remember seeing a picture in a Sunday supplement when I was about sixteen which I could not get out of my head. It showed a heroin addict injecting himself: he had his face covered with one hand while the other hand was pushing a syringe into an arm ribboned with scars. I tore out the photograph and looked at it constantly, until I could not stand it any more; then burnt it. It was black and white and had a caption underneath: 'The routine of addiction.'

I suppose I am a sort of drug addict now. I am addicted to insulin, which I inject several times a day. I do not mind the injections; they have become routine, like cleaning my teeth in the morning. But I think they may be more psychologically oppressive than I admit because there was one brief period when I tried doing without insulin, and though I felt hideously ill, the sense of liberation was like being drunk. It was a short, heady two weeks of freedom.

However, at the beginning I did not know what diabetes would entail, and I looked on a blood test as a new and interesting – though undesirable – experience. It turned out to be very undesirable indeed because I have reluctant veins, which move away from needles, and when they have finally been caught and punctured stop giving blood as soon as they have started. Poor Dr James had a hard time of it and went so far as to give me his hand to squeeze because he said it must be hurting. Finally, after numerous attempts, numerous syringes and lots of pushing and shoving, he got some blood.

I was proud of the bruises this left on my arm and sat with the sleeve of my nightie rolled up, displaying them for all to see. Dr James came back a little while later and asked me how I felt. I gave him one of my grey answers and he said, 'Well, all I can say is you must be exceptionally tough or exceptionally lucky. You've got the highest blood sugar I've ever seen. I can't understand why you're not in a coma.' I swelled with importance and was a bit taken aback when he then asked me how much carbohydrate I ate. This seemed to lower the drama. I had not realised that carbohydrates, along with injections, are the substance of diabetic life. But thinking about Dr James' question, I realised that since I had come back from India I had stopped eating carbohydrates altogether, though I don't know why. I remember Michael once taking me for a drink in a pub and watching me eat the middle of a sandwich and leave the outside.

'You've stopped eating anything carbohydrate. You used to eat potatoes and you don't any more. I wonder if there's something wrong with your brain as well as your spirit. Of course there would be if you deprive it of potatoes.' And off he went on a panegyric on these, the noblest of vegetables.

I suppose it may have been some subconscious survival instinct that had stopped me eating starchy food, which is death to a diabetic not taking insulin. But I doubt it. I had occasional orgies of sweet eating – to satisfy my mother and everyone else who told me to fatten myself up – though I had stopped eating sweets altogether about a month before I came into hospital. I explained to Dr James that this was because it was Lent. He was incredulous.

'I don't know what to say. But it probably saved your life.'

I grinned, feeling somehow as if I had won a victory.

Dr James retired from the fray for a few minutes, leaving me a booklet to read about diabetes. It began with an explanation of what the disease is. Diabetics cannot make their own insulin, which is the stuff which converts carbohydrate into energy; their pancreases stop producing it for some reason and they have to inject animal insulin as a life-saving substitute. Pork and beef insulin are the two types used in Britain. They work rather differently to human insulin, and need to be balanced with controlled doses of carbohydrate to slow them up and stop them working on the vital blood sugar that feeds the brain. If you do not have enough insulin, you do not use up enough sugar and go on feeling thirsty, tired and worn away. This is the condition known as hyper-glycaemia – hyper for short. If you inject too much insulin, and do not compensate by eating enough carbohydrate to slow it up, it uses up not just excess sugar but the necessary sugar that feeds the brain and you feel ill in a quite different and much more dramatic way. This is known as hypoglycaemia (Greek for a shortfall of sugar in the blood) – hypo for short.

Feeling hypo, or having a hypo, is the worst thing about diabetes. But provided it has not gone too far, this condition is easily put right by eating a spoonful of sugar, a biscuit or a piece of bread; anything to give the insulin something other than your brain fuel to feed on. The diabetic ideal is living in the balance between hyper and hypo, avoiding both extremes.

As described in the booklet, in clinical language with clinical descriptions of the extremes, this ideal balance sounded perfectly possible, even easy. The booklet then hurried on to reassure the 'victim' that he or she could still lead an active life, get married; could still, though with problems, have children. For the first time I felt a twinge of misery. I finished the book and phoned home to tell my mother. She was out and my sister took the news, briefly and dispassionately because she was watching the races on television.

Dr James reappeared with a smaller syringe and said he was going to give me some insulin, which would make me feel better. He filled the syringe with something colourless out of a little bottle and injected it into my shoulder.

'It'll start to work fast. You should feel better in about twenty minutes.'

But the only thing I felt was nauseated, and the nurse went and got Dr James, who must have been bored with me by now. He said that I was bound to feel sick as my blood sugar fell from being far too high to being somewhere near normal.

'In fact it may go a bit lower than normal. I've given you a huge shot of insulin and I expect you'll feel ghastly as well as sick in a little while. But never mind. Just call a nurse. You don't mind feeling ghastly, do you?'

I smiled weakly and wondered if anyone had ever thrown a bedpan at Dr James. But I did not feel ghastly, just very tired, and after he had done another blood test at midnight and said it was much better, I told him how grateful I was and rolled over to go to sleep.

It was my first night in a hospital ward and I found it impossible to sleep. It was airless, with barrages of snoring and the night staff constantly to-ing and fro-ing. At about three o'clock the woman in the bed next to me suddenly woke, got up and jumped on to my bed, grabbing hold of my nightie and whispering fiercely about something she had left behind at home and which they would not let her collect; I could not make out what it was. The nurses came running up and tried to calm her down. In the end they gave her a sedative or something and I managed to go off to sleep an hour or two before breakfast.

The next day I was transferred to a side ward because the sister decreed that I was too young to put up with mad old ladies on top of everything else. It was a good move. The side ward had two beds, two basins and a television. There was a woman in her mid-twenties in the other bed who was alternately garrulous and weepy. She told me that she had something wrong with her glands which had made her go off sex, 'right off it, like an old fish. My 'usband don't believe me.' He was in the army and did not visit her at the hospital. She missed him and her little son, who was being looked after by her mother. But she cheered up easily with chatter and television and we got on well. I was just gossiping with her in between blood tests when my mother walked in, looking hot and bothered.

It was lovely to see someone I knew and I told her I felt better and there was nothing to worry about. I sounded like the last page of the diabetic booklet. Dr James came in and I introduced him to my mother. She was tired after the train journey, hot in her overcoat and obviously worried. He worked round the clock and must have been tired too, but he took us into his office and took the time to give us a talk on diabetes.

'I won't pull any punches,' he began, as if it would ever enter his head to do so. 'All the things that go wrong in later life – heart, circulation, kidneys, eyes and so on – are more likely to go wrong in a diabetic like your daughter, go badly wrong – and early.'

My poor mother looked a bit weepy and I put my arm round her, telling her it was all right, while Dr James went inexorably on.

'It's not all right. You're lucky to be alive. I don't think you realise how serious this is. You'll only learn how to live with diabetes if you learn to take it seriously.'

But he was slightly more cheering when he got on to treatment, in which he evidently had complete faith. If I stuck to the rules, I would be able to handle my diabetes without any problems. My mother looked less weepy, though still somewhat overwrought. I took her off to sit on the bed and natter. She went round to my bed-sit and got my nightie and toothbrush for me, and a few books. I told her not to bother to come up again as I would be out soon. I reckoned a day or two in hospital would be enough to cope with diabetes and I phoned them at work to say I would be back soon. I did not have the faintest idea what diabetes was going to do to my life. I had read in the booklet Dr James gave me that once you had it, you had it for life, but that could be true of a runny nose and I did not take it too seriously. I did not understand then that it was not just a life condition, but also a life sentence.

3

That Mighty Joy

It cannot be. Where is that mighty joy
Which just now took up all my heart?
(George Herbert, *The Temper*)

After my mother had gone, I settled down to cope with the two main irritations of hospital life: noise and boredom. It was hopeless trying to read. There was always the noise of a Hoover, polisher or tea trolley rattling round the ward, a conversation between the nurses or the sound of a bedpan being emptied in the sluice-room next door. Then in the rest hour after lunch the noises changed: to a general hubbub of snoring, groaning and calling for nurses.

As an escape, I used to go for walks up and down the corridors, and stand on the bridge that joined two blocks of the hospital. It was encased in glass, about four storeys up above a road, and I used to gaze for hours at the traffic, the people passing by and the fruitseller on the street corner. One day I went up to the chapel on the top floor. Walking up the stairs was the only exercise I was able to take and I enjoyed it. The chapel was bleak, but blessedly quiet; I sat on the floor for a few minutes and could not resist lying down. Moments later I was asleep in front of the altar-step. It happened that the hospital governors were being shown round that day and they came into the chapel while I was there. I opened my eyes and saw a matron, three men and a woman, talking quietly. They took no notice of me, which I thought was so nice of them that I smiled at the woman as she went past on her way out, and she smiled back. When I got back to the ward, the nurse said they had been looking for me to do the inevitable blood test. I explained where I had been and later stole a look at my medical notes, which patients are not supposed to see, and found written under my name: 'Very religious. Spent a long time in the chapel.' This gave me my first real laugh for days.

The general atmosphere was friendly but on the dreary side. There is too much time in hospital, and patients spend it in competitive conversations over who has the worst symptoms and which doctor has the coldest hands. I think that is because I was in a women's ward and women are more critical in hospital than men. They like things done the way they are done at home, and find fault with everything from the temperature of the bath-water to the consistency of the semolina. The boredom is long and exhausting: you get up at an unthinkable hour and there is nothing to pull you out of yourself until bedtime except visitors, who appear like angels and brighten everything during the precious visiting hours.

I loved being visited. Everything from the outside world was a luxury; I loved turning the glossy pages of *Country Life* and *Vogue* and looked endlessly at the daffodils I had been brought. It was late spring and I was inundated with these, my favourite flowers. I was amazed at how quickly people heard I was in hospital and how many of them came to see me or sent presents. I wore myself out talking, then lay and revelled in my flowers, which covered every available surface in the room.

I even liked being visited by doctors and nurses. They were too busy to talk much, but were usually very friendly, and I counted their attentions a welcome break in the noisy indolence that suffocated us all. The Westminster is a teaching hospital and students used to descend at random during the day and ask long lists of prepared questions. They must have been assigned a few patients each to study, and were keen to find out as much as they could. They conversed easily, took the patients' responses very seriously and every so often chased after an answer like a hound after a hare, in case it was something significant that only they had spotted. There was one American student who was especially keen. He was so nervous doing blood tests that his hand shook and he dropped needles on the floor. Then he would apologise and make awkward conversation about his family back home in the States. He asked me if he could come to supper when I got out, and as he was poised above me at the time with a syringe, about to strike, I thought I'd better say yes. His intensity and concern made me feel looked after. He was the only student or doctor who smiled habitually, and whenever he passed the door he would stick his head in and wink.

I was well cared for in the Westminster. Dr James was right when he assured me that I would feel better once I started taking insulin. I had an insulin injection every morning and evening; almost immediately I stopped feeling so tired and stopped drinking and peeing so much.

Then I had my first hypo, something I had been warned about and had read about, but the actual experience was terrifying. Though relatively mild, I will never forget it. I went to Sunday mass in the hospital chapel, which was used by all denominations. It was Palm Sunday. I stood in my dressing-gown with a palm in my hand and heard the priest saying mass but I was miles away from it all. I did not join in the responses, and I could not pray. I just stood there, feeling sadder and sadder, waving my palm about and shivering. I went up to communion and found I was drenched in sweat as

56

well as icy cold. I felt disconnected from everything and after mass wandered vacantly along to the lift, getting out the first time the doors opened. Luckily it was at my floor.

I walked down the corridor to the side ward like a drunk, shaking and dragging my feet. I held on to the hand-rail and could not stop my hand shaking. I got to the ward and lay down on my bed, crying and ignoring my room-mate. I closed my eyes and tears oozed out and rolled down my face. I could not stop them. I stretched my feet taut to try and stop them shaking and felt the skin crack open. A nurse came in and took my pulse, then went and returned with Dr James. He put his hand under my head and said, 'Sit up and drink this.' I tried to move but could not. He and the nurse propped me up and put a mug against my lips. I drank some warm, sweet milk. 'Drink it all,' said Dr James.

I did so and stopped shaking before I had swallowed the last mouthful. I felt better, and smiled.

'Well, now you know. If you ever feel like that again, eat or drink something sweet straight away. Don't go walking around.'

He took a blood test and told me to stay in bed for a bit. I lay there and marvelled at feeling alive again. It was my first taste of a sensation I have had countless times since, in varying degrees according to the severity of the hypo it follows. The worse the hypo, the more intense the joy at coming back to the land of the living afterwards. Most diabetics feel low after hypos, but I feel serene and simply, indomitably happy.

That evening I had less insulin, to avoid another hypo, and became hyper instead; listless, thirsty and endlessly padding along to the lavatory. I gave up trying to sleep and played cards with the night staff. My main worry at that stage was not feeling hypo (I did not know what that could be like at its worst) or hyper (I was used to that); it was having to eat carbohydrate all the time, especially at breakfast. I only had

57

small injections of insulin and only ate what the nurses considered small amounts of carbohydrate to balance them, but to me it was mountainous: two pieces of toast and cornflakes at breakfast, two scoops of potato and some fruit at lunch, two scoops of potato and some ice-cream or fruit at supper.

Carbohydrate is reckoned in 'portions' of ten grams. A scoop of potato is one portion; so is an apple or a glass of pure orange juice. It does not matter in what form you eat the carbohydrate as long as you eat the correct number of portions, and you can swop an apple for a biscuit, or potatoes for bread. The nurse gave me a booklet of carbohydrate 'exchanges', which told me how many portions were contained in every sort of food and drink, from a mug of soup to a bunch of grapes, so that I could learn to exchange them at will. However, as most of the hospital carbohydrate came in the form of potatoes and bread, there was not all that much exchanging I could do to brighten up my diet.

I have always had a good appetite, but I was used to eating when I felt like it, and I never ate breakfast. As I had my biggest insulin injection in the morning, I had to have a big, starchy breakfast, and the nurses dumped trayfuls of bread in front of me which I had no choice but to eat. I learnt quickly that food would never again be just a pleasure, but a medicine, and it was a hard lesson. I chewed mournfully through piles of starch: everything I ate seemed to be white and dull, and by the time I had eaten it I had no room left for anything else.

Worse, though, were the 'snacks' between meals – milk or biscuits, both of which I despised. I was forced to eat biscuits in the middle of the morning, biscuits at tea-time and, supreme horror, hot milk before going to sleep. That it should come to this, I thought: hot milk at bedtime. The first night I was given it, I looked across and saw that my roommate was already asleep, and nipped out to pour my milk down the sink. The lights were out in the ward; it must have been after ten o'clock, and I heard footsteps. I thought it must be the nurse or a domestic coming to collect my mug, and I leapt back into bed. Seconds later the footsteps stopped and Michael appeared at the door.

Visiting hours were generous, and generously interpreted, but by any standards this was an illicit visit. I was overjoyed. He came in, wearing a doctor's white coat which he said he had found on a peg, and carrying a bottle of flowers. There were just two daffodils, all that would fit in the neck of the bottle, and I put them in a vase with some others, while Michael looked disbelievingly at the mug by the basin.

'What's this?'

'Milk.' I could not deny it.

'Holy God.'

He washed out the mug and filled it with water from the bottle. I told him the milk was not my fault, and to use tap water because it would taste nicer.

'It will not,' he said with a smile. 'This is the water of life.'

Ishka baha is Gaelic for the water of life; that is, whisky, or in this case poteen. I sank back on the pillows and drank the whole mugful slowly, sipping ecstatically while Michael swigged it from the neck of the bottle. I used to be rude about Michael's poteen, which tasted like a mixture of fire, acid and mud, but that night it tasted of heaven. It was the water of the other kind of life, the kind I had suddenly lost, a thousand miles away from hot milk, balance and taking care.

The poteen had its usual effect of making my eyes water, my voice husky and my spirits float gently up to careless heights.

'So, creature, how are you? It's a strange place to find you.'

I said I was fine.

'And in yourself?'

In yourself meant 'in spirit', and I answered that this, too, was fine.

59

'Then I've no fear for you.'

He filled the mug again. We discussed the possibility of going out for a game of poker before breakfast but I decided that was impossible. Dr James would come in to do a midnight blood test and I would have to be there. And no sooner had I spoken his name than in he walked, complete with a tray of needles, syringes and tourniquets.

'Are you visiting Teresa? How did you get in? It's long past visiting hours. And where did you get that hospital coat?'

Inspired by the scent of battle, Michael explained that he was indeed visiting me and had chosen a quiet hour so as not to disturb anyone else. He had got in by walking through the door and had found the hospital coat on the hook in the corridor, where he had thoughtfully left his own in temporary exchange, in case anyone needed a coat. I turned my head sideways and chewed the pillow to stop myself laughing. Dr James pulled back his syringe with concentrated fury and was about to stick it in me when he saw the mug in my other hand.

'Put that down.'

I had to reach across him to do so and he sniffed it suspiciously.

'What's in it?' he asked.

'It's a kind of water,' I replied, asking God for forgiveness.

'If you've been drinking, your blood will be full of sugar and this blood test will be a waste of time. I'll have to come back and do another one.'

I thought it was time to apologise, but my efforts were intercepted by Michael, who launched into a Dr James style scientific lecture on the making of alcohol, in which he argued that the conversion of sugar to alcohol is intrinsic, so the consumption of alcohol cannot possibly increase sugar in the blood, only alcohol, which is, of course, greatly to be desired. I sighed. Michael always went just a bit too far.

Dr James finished his blood test before he turned to give

him a piece of his mind, by which time Michael had vanished as blithely as he had appeared, leaving me to listen to the doctor's lecture on my own. I nodded dreamily but did not hear a word. My room-mate snored on while I looked out of the window at London, feeling happy.

In the morning when I cleaned my teeth I saw that Michael had left the empty bottle by the basin. I put a couple of daffodils in it. I was to be allowed outside for the first time so I dressed in a fever of excitement. I walked slowly along the Embankment and back through Smith Square, overcome with how much was going on all around me. There was a bird singing in a tree, and I stopped and listened to it, basking in my short burst of freedom.

I got back to a flurry of tidying and bedmaking as the consultant was coming on his round that morning. I sat on the bed and waited. The consultant was a man called Dudley Hart, short, stout and thinning on top, with a gentle face. He swept round the ward with a flotilla of students and doctors trailing behind him, listening attentively to summaries of each patient's case, asking questions and delivering judgements. The last person he saw in the main ward was an old lady called Miss Archer, with whom I had become friendly, and I wondered what he would say to her.

She was tiny, bright and twisted like a twig by arthritis. She sat out in her chair all day, ate all before her and smiled at everyone. She had arthritis in every joint and could no longer do anything for herself. Up until the week before the only part of her unaffected had been her vision, and she had read continually; books had been her one remaining pleasure in life. But then she had got arthritis in the muscles behind her eyes and could not read any more. Now she sat quite still with her gnarled hands on the table. Whatever could he say to her?

Dr Hart discussed her case briefly then put his hand up to stroke her strands of white hair.

'There's only a certain amount we can do for you, Miss Archer. You know that, don't you?'

She nodded, though her head was bent painfully between her shoulders.

'But I know you of old and you're a fighter, aren't you? God bless you, my dear.'

I asked God to bless them both. He was the old style of doctor, compassionate and stoically humble. I popped in to see Miss Archer a week later, after my discharge, when I had to come back for an out-patients appointment, and gave her a picture book of her beloved London, hoping she would at least be able to see the photos. She was away at X-ray and I left the book with a note, which I suppose someone else had to read to her.

Dr Hart came into the side ward. He smiled at me and listened while Dr James talked about my case, then asked me how I felt. I told him I felt fine and wanted to go home.

'Can she go home, Dr James?' he asked.

'She's a bit unstable.'

'I'm not,' I said indignantly.

Dr Hart smiled again. 'He's talking about your diabetes. It's a medical term, and means your blood sugar goes up and down rather quickly. But I see from your notes that you are described as pleasant and intelligent,' another smile, and a wink from the American student, who had been writing in my notes just before the round began, 'so we'll see what we can do.'

The round was over and the flotilla quickly dispersed. Dr Hart was the last to leave, and just before he went he squeezed my big toe through the bedclothes. It was a small gesture, but one I won't forget. Years later I was listening to a radio programme and one of the speakers was introduced as Dr Dudley Hart, a retired consultant physician and a Christian. He talked about hope against the background of his work, and I remembered his kindness on that round.

Dr James and the Scottish doctor who had admitted me

came to see me afterwards and said I could go home if I promised to go no further than my bed-sit, and to ring that night and say how I was. I dutifully agreed. Then I had to show them that I could inject myself.

Many people practise giving injections on an orange as the skin and pith resist the needle in the same way; once through the tough exterior, the needle slips in. However I had learnt how to do insulin injections the day after being admitted to hospital. The sooner you learn the better, as you then stop being dependent on someone else. It isn't difficult. You get a syringe, fix a needle on the end and inject it through the rubber bung that seals the insulin bottle. The syringe is clearly marked in units so you draw back the plunger until you have as much insulin as you want. If you have an air bubble at the top from drawing the plunger back too quickly, you inject the liquid and the bubble back into the bottle and start again.

You then push the needle under your skin, but not into a vein, at an angle of about forty-five degrees, choosing a well-covered site, such as the stomach, or a thigh, upper arm or buttock. I did not have much flesh anywhere and so had to pinch my skin up to get enough to inject. I also had to push hard at the beginning to get the needle through, as my skin was so dry and tough, but once in, the needle slipped through the flesh, I pushed the plunger home and all the insulin went in. I got the hang of it straight away. However, when I did the injection for Doctors James and Scottish, maddeningly I got the needle in at too acute an angle so the liquid only just got under the skin and stayed there in a bubble. (It is sore when it happens like that but it does not really matter.) The doctors looked at it dubiously.

'You haven't got much technique,' said Dr James, but the Scottish doctor shrugged and said that I would probably get by if I used my head. They pronounced that I could go home that evening. I was thrilled, and got ready hours too soon, to the envy of my room-mate, who lay forlornly on her bed saying that it was all right for some.

Before I left I had to make an out-patients appointment, recite my understanding of diabetes – in particular what I would do if I felt at all hypo – and collect a urine-testing kit, so I could keep a record of the times sugar was present in my urine.

Nowadays all you do is pee on to a dipstick and see if it changes colour. Twelve years ago dipsticks were rare and there was a more involved procedure. You had to pee into a container, transfer five drops into a test-tube, then, using a dropper, add ten drops of water and a tablet. The tablet fizzled up and you had to keep a record of what colour it went: from blue indicating no sugar, through green, greenish yellow to orange at the sugary end of the scale.

The kit I was given came packed in a plastic box about the size of a small camera, with a notebook to record the results. The bottle containing the tablets had to be kept dry. If you kept it in the bathroom and it got damp, the tablets stuck together in an angry lump and turned inky blue. Sometimes when you put them in the test-tube, they smoked as well as fizzled. It was like a malevolent chemistry experiment. Armed with this little kit, I flushed my romantic image of illness down the lavatory in test-tubes of coloured pee, initiating myself into an embarrassing underworld where the hallmarks were how much you weighed and how often you peed, and the virtues were the unspeakable ones of balance and moderation.

But then I had no idea of what diabetes really meant, no notion of how it would affect my life in the long term and no real worries about it. I may even have been a little proud of being a diabetic and looked forward to the sympathy of my family and friends. I said goodbye to Dr James and the nurses, to Mrs Archer and to the other patients and walked out of the hospital with my bag full of syringes, needles, get well cards and leaflets on diabetes. I walked back to my bed-sit, feeling unexpectedly disorientated in the outside world. I wanted to tell every passer-by that I had just come out of hospital, that it might be tea-time for them but it was nearly supper-time for me; my last day in hospital had been a long one and I needed careful handling.

Back in the bed-sit, I found bills in brown envelopes, wilting plants and an empty fridge. It was Maundy Thursday: I had only been in hospital six days but it felt like a little lifetime in itself. I did not want to get back to ordinary life all at once – on my own – over the Easter weekend, so I quickly packed my bag and caught a train home. During the journey, a man seated opposite stared at the bruises on my arm and at my ankles, which still looked like plastic bags full of treacle. I felt extraordinarily tired.

When I got to the station at home I walked through the alleyway to the Catholic church and went to the Maundy evening mass, where my family kept looking round and waving. They were delighted to have me back, and my mother was full of questions, keen to understand everything about diabetes so she could be of help. Doe was quiet and my father was characteristically uninterested in the facts but full of love and sympathy. I injected myself proudly in front of my mother, who wanted to see it done, and ate my twenty grams of carbohydrate for supper. I rang Dr James and told him, without, I am afraid, any pangs of conscience, that I was well and in my bed-sit.

The next day was Good Friday, one of the only two days of fasting and abstinence left in the Catholic Church. I wanted to fast and managed it without going hypo because fasting allows two small meals or collations besides a main meal, which gave me enough starch. The snacks in between I counted as medicinal and therefore allowable. At mass, I stood all through the long gospel of the Passion and felt fine. On Holy Saturday we went to a Benedictine monastery nearby for the Easter Vigil, which starts at midnight and goes on for over two hours. I have always enjoyed this celebration and loved the old monastic chapel where we were all crowded in, choked with incense, standing shoulder to shoulder. I was all right until about half-way through, when I started to feel sad and unsteady. I took some glucose tablets which revived me, and on the grounds that they were medicinal and did not count as breaking the pre-communion fast, went to communion. It was a good Easter.

That evening I had gone upstairs to give myself an injection and my sister – who had been quiet and distant up until then – surprised me by coming into my bedroom to ask if she could watch. Doe looked worried as I pushed the needle into my leg, so I said, 'It doesn't hurt. I can leave it as long as I like and it doesn't hurt,' wobbling the syringe about to prove my point. Doe fainted. Like a tree felled, dead straight. She hit the floor with a tremendous crash and my mother, who thought something must have happened to me, came running upstairs. My brother was visiting us for the day and helped us put Doe on the bed, where she lay unconscious for so long that my mother called the doctor. He came and said she was mildly concussed and should stay in bed for a few hours. He asked me how I was, amused that of the two of us it was Doe who had needed his attention.

When she came round, some minutes later, all Doe could say was, 'Poor Tease' (an affectionate family nickname for me). She repeated it over and over again then asked me why I had injected myself. She knew I was diabetic but somehow or other had shut it out of her understanding. Now that she had taken it in, the realisation had proved too much for her. She lay there, crying quietly, saying, 'Poor Tease.' I was touched beyond words.

That Easter, I experienced the sad pleasure of being specially looked after for the first time. There is no describing how much that kind of care helps. Often it is all people can give you, and it is everything. During my stay, my mother and the old Mother Superior from the convent, Sister Hildegarde, took me to see a country house a few miles away. As we walked round the garden, I started to shake. My mother immediately gave me some biscuits from her pocket; Sister Hildegarde asked me if I was all right and offered to get anything I needed. She is a good cook and spent the rest of the walk discussing recipes and suggesting ways of making sweet puddings without using sugar, which is too concentrated a form of carbohydrate for a diabetic to eat and should only be used in emergencies. The next day I had an Oxford friend, John William, to stay, and he came shopping with me in the village. He was more at home with Greek epics than shopping lists, but he went along the grocer's shelves looking up everything in my diabetic booklet to see how much carbohydrate it contained.

I felt protected, and when John William complimented me on my slim figure, not having seen me since I went to India, I felt chirpy too. I revelled in my slender invalid image. I had four days at home, after which Michael and John William drove me back to my bed-sit, Michael entertaining us with the story of what happened the second time he went to see me in hospital (the first being the poteen incident) and found me gone. The miraculous element that always transfused his life must have taken over, because he ended up having tea with Dr James and giving him the recipe for poteen.

I felt hypo most of the way back to London. Michael suggested a drink, and I wished with all my heart that I could have stuffed diabetes and had one. But instead I had to make him stop in Streatham and buy me a sandwich. Something died inside me, and I celebrated my twenty-second birthday drinking with Michael, knowing that things were going to be different from now on.

4

All the Good Things

And all the good things which an animal likes
Have the wrong sort of swallow or too many spikes.
(A. A. Milne, *The House at Pooh Corner*)

There is no cure for diabetes. Once you have got it, you have got it for life. Anyone can get diabetes. Mild diabetes, which does not require insulin treatment, is common among middle aged, overweight people. But insulin-dependent diabetes can strike anyone at any time, just as it did me. And so, in this chapter, I want to explain what diabetes is, what causes it and how it is treated.

Diabetes is a Greek word which means the passing of water – or, to be more pedantic, a syphon. The ancient Egyptians described a condition characterised by excessive urination as long ago as 1500 BC, in the *Ebers Papyrus*, but it was the Greeks who named it. A Greek physician in the second century, Arataeus of Cappadocia, became positively lyrical about diabetes, enlarging on the name by describing it as 'a melting down of the flesh into water'. The full name for the condition is, in fact, diabetes mellitus, meaning the passing of honeyed water, which distinguishes it from diabetes insipidus, a rare disorder of the pituitary gland also characterised by the passing of water but unrelated to diabetes mellitus.

The ancient Greeks, Indians and Arabs all claim the credit

for having made the unattractive discovery that the water passed by diabetics contained sugar, though an English doctor in the seventeenth century went further than that. His name was Thomas Willis and I read a disgusting account of him heating diabetic urine in test tubes, tasting it on the end of his finger and making his pupils do likewise, to prove there was sugar in it. He made the obvious conclusion that diabetics passed honeyed or sugared water because they could not metabolise honey, sugar or sweet food, and he made them exclude those foods from their diet.

That helped to relieve their symptoms but did not remedy what caused them. It was only in the mid-nineteenth century, when a French scientist called Claude Bernard established the existence of high blood sugar levels in diabetics, that the medical profession got near to understanding what diabetes actually was. It is a deficiency of the insulin hormone, which is produced by the pancreas to metabolise sugar into energy. It can be a relative or an absolute deficiency; mild or severe diabetes, with mild or severe symptoms. Mild diabetes, which can be controlled by diet alone, is much the most common sort, but whether mild or severe, diabetes is always an insulin deficiency.

The connection between diabetes and the pancreas was made in 1889 when two German scientists, experimenting to see what effect the removal of a dog's pancreas would have on its digestion, found that the dog developed diabetes. It panted with thirst, passed sticky urine and died a few hours later in a coma. In a desperate attempt to give diabetics the unknown, vital substance that the pancreas provided, doctors made their diabetic patients eat raw sweetbreads, including pancreas. Diabetic children, emaciated by subsisting on a 400 calorie a day diet with no carbohydrate, had to force down raw, bloody chunks of liver and pancreas. Their plight touched the hearts of the public and research into diabetes was stepped up, until it was interrupted by the First World War.

A young Canadian surgeon, Frederick Grant Banting, was injured in the war and sent back to Canada to continue his medical studies. He was given a laboratory, permission to experiment on dogs, and the services of a twenty-one-year-old assistant called Charles Best.

Between them Banting and Best made the crucial breakthrough. They discovered insulin, which has saved the lives of every severe diabetic from that day to this. There are about six million insulin-dependent diabetics in the world today and they all, including me, owe their lives to Banting and Best's discovery.

It was made in primitive conditions after years of research. The two men ran out of money and were forced to sell their belongings to keep going. At first their experiments were unsuccessful, then one day in 1921 they injected some pancreatic extract into a diabetic dog and its symptoms disappeared. They repeated the experiment on other diabetic dogs and each time succeeded in lowering the animal's blood sugar. They started extracting the juice, which they called insulin, from the pancreases of cattle and pigs.

On January 11th, 1922 insulin was used for the first time on a human being. A fourteen-year-old boy, Leonard Thompson, was in a diabetic coma in a Toronto hospital. As there was no hope for him anyway, they took the chance and gave him a shot of insulin. The response was better than anyone had dared to hope: he came out of the coma immediately and recovered. From that day insulin became the standard treatment for severe diabetes and has been ever since. It is the basic energy hormone and without it the body dies; without enough of it the body deteriorates. Insulin treatment for diabetes is replacement treatment.

Insulin is produced in the pancreas by a group of cells called the Islets of Langerhans, after the German medical student Paul Langerhans who discovered them some years after

Banting and Best's breakthrough. The pancreas is a large, pale yellow gland about six inches by one and a half inches, which lies in the upper abdomen. The islets have three kinds of cells: alpha, beta and delta, and it is the beta cells which produce insulin. In a process which is still not clearly understood even today, insulin enables glucose – released into the blood by the liver – to pass through the membrane of a cell so the cell can burn it up as energy. If there is no insulin, or insufficient insulin, the glucose is not absorbed by the cells and accumulates in the blood.

There are over 600,000 known diabetics in Britain, approximately one per cent of the population, and about eighty per cent of these are only partially deficient in insulin. There are probably about the same number again of undiagnosed diabetics, of whom the vast majority will be mild. The same proportions apply to the world population as a whole.

Mild diabetics are usually over forty years of age and usually – in ninety per cent of cases – overweight. It could be that they develop diabetes because they have been overloading their pancreases with starchy food and not exercising enough to use it up; the result is they cannot produce enough insulin to metabolise the starch. This kind of mild diabetes, also known as adult diabetes, is easily controlled by cutting down on the intake of carbohydrates. There is no need for injections; all these very mild diabetics have to do is to avoid concentrated carbohydrates like sweets and chocolates.

Diabetes is an odd condition. It is personal; as personal as each individual's body, but because it is connected with diet, it also involves friends and family. Nothing can be worse for a diabetic than living with people who are always trying to persuade him to join in the fish and chips or eat just one slice of cake to be like everyone else. Equally, nobody can be more help than those who understand the condition and leave

71

the diabetic to eat a cheese salad unmolested or, better still, keep a weather eye out to make sure there is no cheating with illicit sessions of forbidden starch.

Doctors and dieticians work out how much carbohydrate their mildly diabetic patients can have and how much weight they must lose in order to lighten their pancreatic load. The walls of diabetic clinics everywhere are festooned with literature on diet: food values, respective carbohydrate content and – the only good read of the lot – forbidden foods.

It is up to a mild diabetic to control his own diabetes. If he cheats on his diet, his impaired insulin supply will not be able to deal with it and his blood sugar will go up. If he sticks to his diet, however, his blood sugar should stay near normal. Some mild diabetics are not allowed any carbohydrate at all, but that is unusual. In a grisly way, medicine has its fads like anything else, and 'no carbohydrate' is a sixties fashion. Today's is high fibre, and the more of it the better. The argument is that high fibre carbohydrates provide energy, are easier to absorb than refined ones, and make less demands on insulin. High fibre foods like whole wheat and brown rice have not had the roughage or bran taken out of them and this forms a protective wrapping round the carbohydrate content, thus making its absorption slower and steadier.

Diabetics who were warned off carbohydrates twenty years ago are often encouraged to eat high fibre carbohydrates nowadays. When my diabetes was diagnosed in 1973 I was put on a low carbohydrate diet – just enough to balance the insulin I was taking. Two years ago I saw one of the new wave high fibre doctors who put me on a high fibre, high carbohydrate diet and sent me away with booklets about unpeeled fruit and wholemeal flour.

It was a shock to the system. After a decade of crispbreads, I went to the baker and bought a loaf of wholemeal bread which I not only could, but should, eat. I looked at it every time I went into the kitchen, picking bits of grain off the top, admiring it like a sculpture, before finally cutting the crust off the end and eating it. It tasted fabulous, the first real bread I had eaten for ten years. Now I am sick of bread. You can't win.

However, I am sure that mild diabetics must find their diet more onerous than insulin-dependent diabetics like myself because they do not have injected insulin to help them and so must stay scrupulously within the carbohydrate limits set by doctors and dieticians. In a society obsessively concerned with diet and health, it is tedious beyond measure to be constantly gauging carbohydrate content. It may be healthy but, like most healthy things, it is boring, with only the occasional interesting fact to lighten the darkness, carbohydrate values being a case in point. It was news to me, for example, that fruit is full of it – one glass of orange juice has as much carbohydrate as a thick slice of bread; one apple has as much as two biscuits. I was given a booklet on the amount of carbohydrate in proprietary foods which was an eye-opener. All the different makes of yoghurt were listed and how much carbohydrate and sugar each contained; some had three times as much as others. One well known manufacturer of sausages, pork pies and cold meats has so much carbohydrate in all its foods that they must be made of meat and breadcrumbs, fifty-fifty.

My curiosity was awakened and I wrote to Brown and Polson, who make blancmange powder – a product mysteriously excluded from the leaflet, and one of my favourite desserts – to ask them how much carbohydrate each envelope of powder contained. They wrote back by return. It was a charming letter with exact details of carbohydrate, calories and all the other contents, advice on sugarless recipes for diabetics and an invitation to come and meet their dietician, to see how their products were made and discuss the research they were doing into 'sugar alternative' foods. I have bought Brown and Polson's blancmange ever since.

Some mild diabetics are so deficient in insulin that they cannot metabolise even a low carbohydrate diet and have to take pills to stimulate their insulin production. Like all the diabetic life-savers, these pills are a modern discovery and like so many life-saving discoveries, such as penicillin, this one was made by accident. In 1954 two Germans were experimenting with sulpha drugs, used in the treatment of bacterial infections, and noticed that patients taking the tablets suffered a drop in blood sugar levels. And sulpha drugs, or sulphonylureas, have been used to lower the blood sugar of mild diabetics to normal levels ever since. They work on two fronts, pepping up the beta cells in the pancreas to produce more insulin and simultaneously inhibiting the release of glucose from the liver. In conjunction with diet and exercise they should be enough to make the mild diabetic metabolise food into fuel normally.

I was put on sulpha drugs once, but they did not make me normal. That is because I am what is known as a juvenile diabetic, totally dependent on injected insulin, as I cannot produce any of my own. The sulpha treatment was a shot in the dark and was tried just in case I was producing a little bit of insulin and could be coaxed into producing enough to live on. I took so little insulin that the doctors I saw in out-patients at the Westminster thought it was worth a try. They warned me that the treatment probably would not work, but I had no qualms in trying as I had been injecting myself with insulin twice a day and the possibility of escaping that was irresistible.

I took a tiny white tablet called Glibenclamide morning and evening and ate meals without any carbohydrate. I went on holiday to Ireland and had a lovely time walking, picking raspberries and rowing on the lakes near Loch Derg. The more exercise you take, the more sugar you use up, and the more chance you give the drugs to be effective. Exercise is partner to diet in the treatment of diabetes. In fact it is such an efficient partner that mild diabetics can run themselves short of sugar if they exercise too much. I exercised until I was dropping but became steadily more sugary nevertheless. The freedom from injections was bliss itself, although I got back to England a fortnight later tired and thirsty, and longing like a junkie to get back to the needle.

An absolute insulin deficiency like mine is called juvenile diabetes because it usually develops in childhood, and almost always in people under the age of forty. It means you have to inject insulin to stay alive and is consequently a much more serious condition than mild diabetes. It is a different proposition. Speaking from the heights – or depths – of insulin-dependent diabetes, I sometimes cannot help but consider the other sort of diabetes not worthy of the name. The difference is not so much in the condition, though they are different in degree, as in the treatment. Insulin is as dangerous as the condition it treats. It is a life-saving peril.

Before insulin was discovered by Banting and Best, the only treatment for diabetes was diet, which kept life going, skeletonous and dismal, until the inevitable end. My mother's grandfather was diabetic and died a typical pre-1922, pre-insulin death. He lay on a couch for ten years, drinking tea, too tired to do anything except pee. But I was lucky. I was born the right side of that magic year. And now, sixty years later, insulin production has been organised to perfection. The pancreases of pigs and cows are removed when the animals are slaughtered, and sent to insulin laboratories where they are pressed to extract the life-saving hormone, which is then purified. Pure it may be but for me nothing can hide its horrible, gross animality. I am only alive because I inject myself with a dead pig's hormones, and that is not a genteel thought.

75

I read a story recently which brought home to me more vividly than ever before how bestial insulin is, and how fortunate it is that that is the case. You can grow to accept anything if your life depends on it; I hate insulin but I owe it my life, so I love it too, and identify passionately with the heroine of this tale.

In 1941 a diabetic Czech American woman called Eva Saxl was living with her husband in Shanghai. When the Japanese moved in, she rushed out, with the other diabetics, to buy up all the available insulin, knowing they might not be able to get any more for a long time. She rationed her supply as carefully as she could, ate quantities of Chinese herbs reputed to have healing powers and avoided carbohydrates altogether. But by 1943 she was down to her last bottle of insulin. Her husband, Victor, was frantic. He persuaded local doctors to lend him every medical book in which there was a reference to the making of insulin. In one of them, *Beckman's Internal Medicine*, he found a detailed description of Banting and Best's discovery.

Victor persuaded a Chinese chemist who tested food and drink samples from street stalls to let him use his rudimentary municipal laboratory and equipment to try to make insulin. Victor Saxl was a textile engineer who knew nothing about chemistry or medical technology, but he vowed he would succeed in making insulin and so save Eva's life. He sent her down to the local slaughterhouse early each morning with their Chinese cook, to snatch up the pancreas of any big animal newly slaughtered; usually a water buffalo, occasionally a pig. She put it in a wide necked thermos flask and took it by rickshaw to the Chinese chemist's laboratory, where she ground it up in the kitchen meat grinder. Victor then killed any poisons the pancreas might have contained by heating, freezing and treating the minced-up morsels with alcohol.

When Victor had successfully given a trial injection of the resulting dark-brown liquid to a rabbit, he brought a syringe into the room where Eva was lying on a couch. He kissed her and said, 'Eva, I love you,' injected the home-made insulin into her and ran out of the room in tears. Eva drank some tea, then suddenly jumped up and said, 'It helped.'

For almost three years Eva and other diabetics in Shanghai lived on Victor Saxl's home-made insulin. When the Americans liberated the city, she went with five others to see a US Marine medical officer to try to obtain some standard insulin. The officer opened the door of a fridge to reveal rows and rows of little bottles full of standard, purified, colourless insulin.

'What type and strength do you want?' he asked, and the six of them burst into tears.

When first marketed in 1923, commercial insulin was produced by methods more sophisticated but essentially similar to Victor Saxl's, using the pancreases of cattle or pigs. One of the modern trade names for this first, unmodified insulin is Actrapid, because it acts rapidly, lowering the blood only minutes after injection. Its peak action is two to four hours after injection and it peters out about two hours after that. Because of its short life, it has to be injected several times a day and manufacturers nowadays often add substances, especially zinc, to slow up and prolong its action. There are more than a dozen kinds of beef and pork insulin available today, most of them with added zinc and with active lives varying between eight and thirty-six hours. Some diabetics take a combination of the quick and slow acting insulins; the quick to keep blood sugar down after meals and the slow to keep it down the rest of the time.

I was started off on the old fashioned quick-acting sort, injected twice a day; before breakfast and before supper. But the evening dose did not last through the night and I used to wake up full of sugar in the mornings. I have changed insulins several times since then and have also tried several different combinations. The possible permutations are endless.

Diabetics who respond well to insulin and settle down to a fixed dose and fixed scheme of injections are known as stable diabetics. Most insulin-dependent diabetics are stable, though even the most stable of them may have to change their regime slightly from time to time: the factors affecting blood sugar, and the amount of insulin needed, are legion. The most important of them are age, illness, work, stress, shock, exercise, heat, mood, sex and hormones. That does not leave much out.

At the other extreme, diabetics who respond erratically to insulin, with unpredictable ups and downs in blood sugar, are known as brittle diabetics. They may have to change their injection pattern and dosage fairly often. Some diabetics are brittle for no apparent reason. I am one of those. Some are exceptionally sensitive to one particular affecting factor: others are alternately stable and brittle. Injected insulin is volatile stuff, not least in its relationship with the human body. It acts as a substitute for the insulin the body fails to produce, but that is produced on demand and it is impossible to achieve the same natural, self-adjusting level with injected insulin. In addition, animal insulin also works differently from the human variety. The best that can be done is to find a dosage and injection scheme which keeps a diabetic midway between the extremes of hyperglycaemia and hypoglycaemia. Unfortunately this ideal middle ground has always eluded me, though I am always willing to try a new approach. A doctor recently said that the perfect adage for brittle diabetics like me was 'The triumph of hope over experience,' Dr Johnson's famous dictum about second marriages. I am prepared to keep on hoping.

In Germany, where diabetes is treated with meticulous rigour, brittle diabetics are sometimes put on five or six injections a day, each jab containing enough insulin for the next few hours. The amount required is gauged by pricking the finger before each injection to test the blood sugar level. But for all that, there is no hard evidence to suggest that diabetic control is any better in Germany than in Britain, where most people just do the occasional blood test when they feel unwell. All things considered, I think there is much to be said for taking it easy when the going is hard.

For there is no doubt that the diabetic experience is often unpleasant. In the past it was also occasionally horrific for those who became sensitised to insulin. Their injection sites grew red and painful as they built up more and more anti-bodies to insulin, until they became immune. It was a rare problem but a frightening and potentially fatal one. The only action possible was to change to insulin from a different animal and pray that one did not react badly to that too. Or rather, that was the only action to take until two years ago, when an American company, Eli Lilly, announced that they were beginning mass production of genetically engineered human insulin.

This was the first commercial application of the discovery of the DNA genetic code and has resulted in bio-synthesised human insulin. In layman's terms, a bacterium is injected with the DNA code for the manufacture of human insulin which it then starts to make. This is a staggeringly complicated and immensely costly process but the result for the diabetic is gloriously simple: insulin which cannot be rejected. That crucial fact apart, it is little different from animal insulin, except for the enormous expense of manufacture. And because of the cost, only those who are having trouble with their animal insulin are encouraged to try it. Human insulin is still not the same as an individual's own natural insulin because it cannot be produced as needed: the dangers of over

79

and under dosage remain ever present, and it still has to be injected.

Not even the Germans have found a way of taking insulin without injections. It cannot be taken by mouth because it is a protein and would therefore be destroyed by the digestive juices. Until 1922 you died if you were severely diabetic; until someone finds some other way, you now inject yourself every day of your life instead.

You choose a different place for each injection or, in diabetic jargon, rotate the sites, because if you keep using the same one it becomes bruised and swollen. My left arm is permanently swollen at the top because I am right-handed and used to do a lot of injections into my left arm. I stopped using that site a year ago, in the vain hope that the swelling might go down, and I now inject myself up and down my thighs, up, down and across my stomach and buttocks and, if I am feeling clever, left-handed into my right arm. I am covered with bruises, however much I rotate the sites, but they fade and I do not mind them too much. I mind the swellings more, especially on my thighs, which have come to look like blotchy puff pastry. I try to keep them covered up.

Syringes and needles are supplied free by the National Health Service, but they are not ideal because they are made of glass and have to be stored in a plastic tube full of surgical spirit to keep them sterile. Before using the syringe, you have to wash the spirit off, which means you have to find a tap. If it is not properly rinsed the injection stings savagely and creates a red sore patch around the site. In theory you should also boil the syringe once a week to make doubly sure it is sterile; but after boiling it a couple of times in cabbage water by mistake, I gave up. The hygiene-conscious Americans are advised to bake their syringes in tinfoil once a week but enough is enough and that is too much; I would never be able to do it without adding salt and pepper.

There are several kinds of plastic syringe you can buy and I prefer these because they are 'dry'. They come in sealed sterile plastic envelopes and you can use them on the spot. Again, in theory they should be used once, then thrown away because they are no longer sterile, but they are too dear for that and a lot of doctors agree that they can be used until they are blunt.

In the old days insulin was available in 10, 20, 40 or 80 strengths but quite recently its production went metric and it is now available only at 100 strength. It has taken over a year to effect the change-over and an additional delaying factor has been that different areas started to implement it at different times. But it is a great improvement. Now syringes hold half or 1 ml of insulin, with the milligrams divided into marked units. Each unit on the syringe corresponds to a unit of insulin. Measuring the right amount into the syringe is thus simplified although a mistake in measuring the 100 strength insulin is ten times as serious as a mistake in measuring the 10 strength kind.

There are various syringe elaborations to fit the needs of all sorts of diabetics: one is in the shape of a pen with a dial that fills it with the required amount of insulin, for easy use during the day; one clicks every time it is drawn back one unit, for the use of diabetics with eye problems; one shoots insulin in like a gun. Bad eyesight is one of the commonest side-effects of diabetes and the clicking syringe sounds like a good idea. But the snag is that you often get air bubbles in the syringe when you pull back the plunger, and if you cannot see properly you would not be able to tell whether one of your clicks was an air click or an insulin click.

I once met a man who works for one of the big insulin manufacturing firms and asked him why insulin was not packed in bottles with white rubber tops to replace the brown rubber bungs they have at the moment, which are hard for people with eye problems to see. He said that it was

81

one of those absurd things: no more than custom. I then asked why insulin was not packed in shatter-proof bottles, as it is expensive and you have only to drop one bottle to lose pounds worth of insulin. He said that insulin was a protein and might react against plastic. In that case, I suggested, why not put a plastic coating round the glass bottles? He shrugged; again, it was just custom. Maybe it suits the manufacturers for bottles to get broken, so they can sell more, but it seems to me a needless and expensive waste.

National Health needles are as maddening to use as National Health syringes. They are about half an inch long, like all diabetic needles, and made entirely of metal. You are supposed to use them until they get blunt, keeping them in the same spirit as the syringe. I must have a tough skin, though, because I can hardly get a metal needle through it once, pushing hard, let alone for a second or third injection. I prefer the disposable needles you buy at the chemist which are expensive, fine, sharp and easy to push in. They have plastic hilts which fit the end of the syringe better than the National Health metal hilts; the latter slip off and leave the needle embedded in your flesh and the insulin pouring out of the headless syringe. Disposable needles should be used once and thrown away, although I – and most other insulin-dependent diabetics – use them anything up to a dozen times.

For the last two years or so almost all the disposable syringes on the market have had fixed instead of detachable needles. They are good syringes and draw up and down evenly. Another plus is their wonderfully sharp needles, only about a quarter of an inch long, which you inject vertically, all the way in, without having to worry about getting the right angle or avoiding veins. My only complaint is that you cannot take the needle off when it is blunt and go on using the syringe, though in any case the markings rub off the syringe after four or five goes. More frivolously, not being able to take the needle off means you cannot use the syringe to ice cakes when you have finished using it for injections.

I am loath to be too serious about diabetes. I was bound to lose the happy ignorance I had when I left hospital after my diagnosis, but I do not like knowing more than I need to about it. I have had to learn more than I ever wanted to in order to write this book, but then I have promised myself that the moment I finish I shall let all the extraneous facts fade from my consciousness. I prefer it that way.

5

The Pity

And a chill shiver takes me as she sings
The pity of unpitied human things.
(Arthur Symons, *To Yvette Guilbert*)

Diabetic control is all about balance. Whether you eat or fast, lie in bed or take exercise, you must always aim to achieve a balance between too much and too little sugar. Of the two extremes too little sugar is the more immediately dangerous and to avoid it you have to eat some carbohydrate after every insulin injection; that's a hard and fast rule. If you use quick-acting insulin you have to eat it quickly; if you use slow-acting insulin you have more leeway. But it is still just as important to eat it, to slow the insulin up. If you do not, the insulin will devour all your blood sugar when it reaches its peak, which may be as much as eighteen hours later, depending on the type of insulin injected. You are never free to skip a dose of starch any more than you are free to eat too much of it. You can never play fast and loose with insulin – that is the meanest thing about diabetes – but perhaps meaner still is the fact that insulin often plays fast and loose with you.

The rate at which insulin is absorbed into the bloodstream can vary as much as fifty per cent from site to site and day to day. If you inject it into your arm then walk to work after breakfast, it may be absorbed quickly and you will arrive

84

at work feeling hypoglycaemic. If you inject it into your stomach and sit and read the newspaper after breakfast, it may be absorbed slowly and by mid-morning you will feel hyperglycaemic. Other factors which can affect insulin's action are legion: fat mops up insulin so fat people need more than thin people. Illness nearly always raises blood sugar and you need more insulin, just as exercise lowers blood sugar and you need less. Researchers giving the same people in perfect health the same dose of insulin two days running under the same conditions, in the same temperature, and eating the same food, found their blood sugar level in each case much higher one day than the other – but higher by different amounts and on different days. In an organism as intricately and sensitively complex as the human body, insulin can wreak havoc.

The tiniest bit too much insulin and you go hypoglycaemic. Ask any insulin-dependent diabetic what the worst thing is about diabetes and I guarantee that the answer will be, 'Going hypo.' In its mild forms it makes you tremble and sweat; you feel restless and dis-coordinated; extreme hunger pains stab your stomach and a manic misery plummets you down into the pit of despair. All the blood drains out of your face, which can go chalk white in a matter of seconds, and becomes drenched with sweat. And all for lack of a little bit of sugar.

The brain feeds exclusively on sugar. When it runs out of that it cannot burn anything else to compensate and the body and mind progressively break down, starting with the nervous system, hence the trembling and sweating. One of the worst features of hypoglycaemia is fear; a blanket of nervous fear which grows into dread and – unless you can reverse the hypo – ends in either frantic convulsions or sleepy withdrawal; both of them are a prelude to unconsciousness.

Hypos are easily cured. It is hard to believe that such a

dangerous and often spectacular disorder is put right by swallowing a lump of sugar. Or a biscuit, sandwich, piece of cake or sugary drink; anything that will quickly provide that vital bit of glucose.

There is no one standard level of blood sugar necessary for health. It varies with each individual, with diet, exercise and all the other affecting factors. But it is generally accepted that the minimum level of blood sugar required by an adult is 3.5 millimoles per litre, and the maximum about 8 millimoles per litre, though after eating, a healthy blood sugar level could be as high as 10 or 12 millimoles per litre. Brittle diabetics are given packets of test strips to gauge their blood sugar level so they can top it up if it has fallen low. You prick your fingertip with a needle and put a drop of blood on the end of the test strip. After a minute you wipe off the excess blood and after another minute you look and see what colour the tip has turned. The colours are two-tone and range from cream and very pale turquoise when your blood sugar is down below rock bottom at 1 mmol per litre, through biscuit and bright turquoise when it is normal at up to 7 mmol per litre, then through assorted shades of greenish blue and grey, which means it is over 10 mmol per litre. At the extreme of fearsome dark aquamarine and navy blue, your sugar level is up to 44 mmol per litre and you are lucky to be conscious to see the test stick.

In the long term, high blood sugar levels are destructive because they damage your heart, eyesight and kidneys; in the short term they just make you feel oppressed. But the opposite, hypoglycaemia – low blood sugar – is more apocalyptic. It damages the brain and if sufficiently serious and not reversed, can destroy it. However, you can usually feel a state of mild hypoglycaemia coming on and eat something starchy to redress the balance. Usually, but not always. You can be very mildly hypoglycaemic without realising; feeling irritable, dreary and haphazard for hours at a time. If you let that happen often, your brain begins to lose so many cells that its defences are weakened and you drift into more serious hypoglycaemia without noticing.

Until a couple of years ago I used to know when I was going hypo and took evasive action. But nowadays my hypos are like going over the edge of a cliff; I miss all the symptoms of the mild stage and go straight into the severe stage, where the brain falls headlong into collapse.

The symptoms of hypoglycaemia, mild or severe, are hard for outsiders to recognise. In a mild hypo, a person can seem to be behaving quite normally, though slightly off-centre, tipsy or bizarre. If people do suspect there is something wrong and offer you some sugar, you almost always refuse it because your brain is not working properly and you do the opposite to what you should do. If you are too far gone to help yourself, the best thing for people to do is force something sugary – food or drink – into your mouth. If they do that you revive at once. Dextrose tablets are ideal because even if you have lost consciousness, they can be held against the inside of your cheek where they dissolve instantly and are quickly absorbed into the system.

Severe hypoglycaemia has a host of symptoms, many of them similar to those of the mild form. You feel tired, slow and dizzy. It is impossible to concentrate. You cannot remember anything; in a bad hypo not even who you are, what you are doing and how to do it, including something as instinctive as walking. You see double, your speech is slurred, you shake and reel about. Given these symptoms it is not surprising that hypoglycaemic diabetics are often arrested for suspected drunkenness, especially as they tend to be aggressive and hit out. The whole pattern of behaviour becomes uncharacteristic and grotesque. You are confused and hideously miserable. You feel icy cold, your blood pressure drops and your pulse becomes hit and miss. It is a relief to lose consciousness.

When hypoglycaemia reaches that stage, you need a doctor or hospital attention fast. A fifty per cent glucose solution is injected into the veins and you come round straight away. Alternatively a small syringe of a protein hormone called glucagon can be administered, which is simpler because it does not have to be given intravenously; under the skin will do. Glucagon stimulates the glucose-holding organs, especially the liver, to release their store of glucose and raise your blood sugar level. It takes ten to twenty minutes to work and as soon as you come round you should eat as much as you can force down, to refuel the glucose-holding organs. A doctor generally gives glucagon injections but anyone will do. Some brittle diabetics are given a vial of glucagon on prescription to keep in the household fridge for use in an emergency.

The worst time to go hypo is at night: you can slip into a coma without waking up. You then have to rely on someone finding you and giving you some sugar, or on the insulin wearing off so you can pull out of it on your own. But that can take hours, and it inevitably leaves you feeling on the other side of death.

It is little wonder that brittle diabetics live in terror of hypo-glycaemia, to the extent that some of them purposely take too little insulin and keep their blood sugar a bit high. Doctors are sympathetic to that: many of them advise it. But only within strict limits and under strict supervision.

For even mild hyperglycaemia over a period of years leads to trouble. The body cells cannot absorb glucose so they burn fat as fuel instead. Sometimes so much fat is burnt that as well as severe weight loss a kind of acid is deposited in the blood in the form of ketones, a by-product of burning fat. Ketones are poisonous in large quantities and untreated diabetics sometimes have so many in their blood that their breath smells acidic or fruity, like over-ripe apples, or, as

Dr Hart at the Westminster described it to me with characteristic kindness, like new mown hay.

Excess of ketones to this degree is called ketoacidosis or ketonaemia and unless the blood sugar level is drastically reduced with insulin, it leads to coma and, in a matter of hours, death. I had been teetering on the brink of a ketoacidocic coma when I was diagnosed. I was lucky. Mild diabetics never reach that stage unless they break all the rules; they have enough insulin to metabolise at least some of their glucose.*

A severe diabetic can also burn protein as well as fat in the search for fuel, which a mild diabetic does not. When protein is lost like this, muscle and other tissues are weakened and the whole fabric of the body is undermined. That is the medical explanation of what happens. But from personal experience I know that diabetic tiredness is impossible to describe. It is too absolute for words. It makes a coma or a coffin, or both, seem like a logical progression and you fall quiescently asleep at every opportunity.

Mild diabetics feel tired too, of course, but not in the same way; they also feel thirsty and pee a great deal but not to the same extent. It is just this soft, slow and moderate nature of their symptoms which makes mild diabetes so hard to diagnose. Often sufferers are only discovered when they go to their doctor with some other complaint or explain that their extremities frequently feel numb or are afflicted with pins and needles.

Loss of feeling in the feet sometimes points to poor circulation and suggests that the patient has blood vessel trouble. Although the exact relationship between blood vessel damage and diabetes is unclear, it is nevertheless certain that such a relationship does exist. High blood sugar causes fatty-fibrous lesions which clog up, or in medical terminology occlude,

* Because of this fact mild diabetes is sometimes called ketosis-resistant or nonketotic diabetes.

the arteries so oxygen does not get round the body. Narrow clogged up arteries and thick sugary blood can affect both the large blood vessels, especially those in the heart, brain, hands and feet, and the small blood vessels, especially those in the kidneys and the eyes. In developed countries half the deaths of diabetics are related to heart disease which may be accompanied by high blood pressure. Consequently a diabetic weighing an ounce over his recommended body weight is pounced upon by doctors and dieticians to be dragooned into dieting, though this is not easily accomplished when you have to eat biscuits all day long.

My feet only go numb intermittently and then the numbness does not last long. It is worse in my hands which, I am told, is the opposite to usual, but then I am half-Irish. Before I was diagnosed a diabetic, my feet went numb for days at a time and my fingers were always cold and yellow. This condition is known as neuropathy and losing the ability to sense the onset of a hypo is a form of autonomic neuropathy.

The danger is that you cannot feel cuts and injuries, which get infected quickly and develop into athlete's foot or gangrene. You are supposed to wash your feet in warm, not hot, water with mild soap. No hot water and no washing up in detergent. No bath salts, no wrinkles in your tights, no nice, uncomfortable shoes and – a sin against summer which surely no one can obey – no bare feet. Diabetic clinics always have a sprinkling of patients in wheelchairs with one or both feet cut off because they have had gangrene.

I knew someone that happened to. He was a professor at Cambridge, where I was doing some research a few years ago and where painful feet from gout, a surfeit of port and rich food at college dinners, were commonplace. Jack's toe began to hurt and his doctor diagnosed gout. The pain shot up his leg and within the week they had cut it off at the knee, pronouncing him both gangrenous and diabetic. Jack had survived World War Two in the tank corps, against all odds; he had been through every horror, and I think he felt that his life was out of his hands. If God, or fate, wanted him to live, he would. His own efforts in that direction were insignificant.

Jack came back from the hospital to new rooms in Trinity on the ground floor, where he hobbled about on a tin leg and ate cherry cake if he felt like it. He was not over-indulgent but neither was he over-strict. He loved whisky, which I used to drink with him late at night when his was the only light left on in Great Court. He would read Byron's letters and ask me to go through his evening post, throwing away all the brown enveloped letters and giving him the hand-written ones to read. Whisky is no worse for diabetes than any other spirit but it is still risky. It does not contain much sugar because that has all been turned into alcohol but it contains a wicked number of calories. Like all alcohol. It sends the blood sugar sharply up then slowly but surely down, destabilising the diabetes.

Jack drank whisky in quite small amounts but rather fre-quently. I do not know whether this was the cause or not, but something made him worse all of a sudden and he got an ulcer on his remaining leg. Ulcers and abcesses used to mean automatic amputation but today they can often be healed with antibiotics and careful foot care. Jack was beyond that, though. I had left Cambridge and was living in Oxford by the time I heard about the problems with his remaining leg, but as soon as I got the news, I leapt on a coach and went to see him in Addenbrooke's Hospital.

He had a room of his own with the light pouring in through big glass windows. It gave him a deathly colouring. I could not see his leg because it was under the bedclothes and I could not talk to him much because he had someone with him and was tired out from too many visitors. I gave him a thriller to read and squeezed his hand. He looked horribly jaded. The minute I was outside the door, I regretted that I had not kissed him on top of his shiny bald head, but I had not liked to with his rather formal visitor there.

A few weeks later I got a note from the senior tutor at Trinity telling me that Jack had died. They had let him out of hospital when they could not do any more for him; presumably the poison from the ulcer had spread all through his body. His heart and kidneys had failed. It was a terrible death. The porters told me afterwards they could hear him screaming in Neville's Court, the other side of college.

Jack's funeral was on a wet, bitter March day, with rain lashing across the long line of fellows in their gowns and mortar boards who stood behind his coffin. They sang the *Nunc Dimittis* before taking him out of Great Gate for the last time. When I go back to Cambridge now, I look to the left crossing Great Court because I cannot bear to look over to Jack's rooms, where the curtains were always drawn together and the lamp was always on. Now, whenever I see patients in diabetic clinics with their feet wrapped in dressings and loose socks, I think of Jack and wish I had kissed him while I had the chance.

It was kidney disease that finally killed him. Next to the heart and brain, the kidneys are the most vulnerable to diabetic blood vessel damage. The blood vessels narrow as they filter the excess glucose out of the system and, occluded with fatty deposits, they degenerate. Water and sugar accumulate in the blood and proteins seep through the filters, causing the face and ankles to swell. It is called nephropathy or nephrotic syndrome. Jack suffered a vicious attack of it in the last few days of his life and I am glad I was not there to see it.

The other small blood vessel trouble that frequently affects diabetics is eye disease or retinopathy, and unlike kidney disease this can be directly attributed to high blood sugar. The other sprinkling you see in diabetic clinics besides people in wheelchairs are people with white sticks; diabetes is the leading cause of adult blindness in the United Kingdom. Though only about two per cent of diabetics become totally blind, many more become partially sighted.

Poor diabetic control, especially at the beginning, bodes badly for eyesight, though there are some doctors who think it is the *duration* of diabetes, not the relative efficiency of its containment, that causes the trouble. Generally, I do not think much about the possible problems awaiting me in my diabetes but I do momentarily feel my heart skip a beat every time I have my eyes tested. I have been diabetic for twelve years, all twelve of them poorly controlled, and so far I have never had any trouble with my eyes, except for double vision when I go hypo (which is caused by muscle failure and quickly set right by eating some sugar). Last time I had my eyes tested, the doctor told me that women's eyes generally last longer than men's before they begin to deteriorate. I said an extra prayer while he shone his ophthalmoscope into my eyes and another when he switched it off and said they were all clear.

An ophthalmoscope is a bright magnifying light which illuminates the retina at the back of the eye. The retina is served by tiny blood vessels and covered with nerve cells connecting the optic nerve to the brain. In diabetics, high blood sugar enlarges these tiny blood vessels until they break open and haemorrhage, thus damaging the retina. An ophthalmoscope shows up these haemorrhages and also the new blood vessels the body manufactures to replace them, which tend to grow forward into the clear jelly of the eye, causing more haemorrhages and retinal detachment. Blood from haemorrhages can also leak into the eyeball jelly and has to be removed: a surgeon slits the eyeball, takes the jelly away, and replaces it with a salt solution.

Both glaucoma (caused by increased pressure on the eyeball), and cataracts are also more prevalent in diabetics than non-diabetics. The early stages of glaucoma are marked by blurred vision and coloured blobs but if reported early enough, the condition can be treated with drugs. However, it can also happen suddenly, with a burst of acute pain, and then it becomes impossible to treat with drugs or surgery. (Cataracts, caused by sugar leaking on to the lens of the eye, are removed by surgery.)

Eye haemorrhages used to be irreversibly cumulative but now they are sealed off by a form of laser treatment called photocoagulation. A laser surgeon dilates the eyes with drops and fires a narrow beam of intense light at the haemorrhages, which cauterises and stops them leaking. This treatment slows up, and can even prevent, diabetic blindness.

It is typical of diabetes that an unbalanced diet should work its way into eye trouble. As if one needed it. Too much fat in the diet, or too much sugar (which in turn causes high levels of fat in the blood), can leave deposits of fat and protein called exudates on the retina. This is often the first sign that someone has diabetes and treatment, in inimitable diabetic style, is by a low fat, low carbohydrate diet and weight loss.

Once you have retinopathy, there is no evidence that good diabetic control stops its progress, which I suppose is a perverse consolation; as far as your eyes are concerned, you might as well eat sweets until you are sick. And I, for one, would start with iced caramels.

But it is not worth it. The onset of all blood vessel diseases caused by diabetes is linked with high blood sugar, and each is serious. Hyperglycaemia is slowly dangerous, but it is always dangerous in the end. In various complicated ways it is linked with the nervous system, which it slowly destroys. The involuntary or autonomic nervous system controls all bodily functions which we do not think about, like the heart beating, and it is damaged when the blood sugar level is consistently high enough to disintegrate the fatty covering on nerve fibres.

Another complication caused by poor blood sugar control – and the one which diabetics understandably tend to keep quiet about – is impotence and, related to that, retrograde ejaculation. This latter complaint seems to me to sum up the psychology of diabetes, being humiliating, undignified and cruelly absurd. Men with poorly controlled diabetes are often unable to have an erection or, if they do manage, then they find themselves ejaculating backwards into the bladder instead of through the penis. It embarrasses me just to write about it; heaven knows what it is like for the victims. Mercifully, women's sex lives do not seem to be affected by diabetes, so I am spared writing about that (though some American research claims to have discovered that diabetic women have fewer orgasms). In any event, all these sexual problems are the direct result of high blood sugar and, in theory at least, can be put right with better blood sugar control.

So can the purely nervous problems that diabetes causes: high blood pressure, dizziness, diarrhoea and, somehow the unkindest of all, bad teeth and gums. Last time I was in hospital the young woman in the bed next to me lay with the sheet over her mouth the whole time because she had developed abscesses on her gums and all her teeth had been taken out.

The most important time to keep blood sugar under control is during pregnancy. Before the discovery of insulin, diabetic women hardly ever managed to get pregnant and those who did usually died as a result. The extra hormones produced during pregnancy work against insulin and raise the blood sugar level. A lot of otherwise healthy women become mildly hyperglycaemic during pregnancy and feel tired, thirsty and depressed. Their best course is to do the same as diabetic women: exercise frequently and eat as little starch as possible.

By about a month after delivery, blood sugar should return to normal but with some women it remains high and they become diabetic. The likelihood of this increases with each pregnancy, especially for overweight women, but the diabetes is usually mild.

Diabetes can only be controlled with sulpha drugs after, and never during, pregnancy and breast feeding, because they can penetrate the placenta and cause congenital defects in the foetus. The drugs can also pass through into the mother's milk and cause hypoglycaemia in the baby. Mildly diabetic women who cannot control their blood sugar with diet alone may have to take a bit of insulin during pregnancy and the breast-feeding months, but with luck should be able to give it up afterwards.

In England, pregnant diabetics may be fussed over, with endless blood and urine tests, visits to diabetic clinics and weighing and diet sessions, but in Germany their lives are even more strictly controlled; they might as well take their belongings and some good books and move into hospital for the duration. Despite obvious drawbacks, all this care and attention has done away with the pressure applied till very recently on diabetic women to avoid the risk of pregnancy altogether. There are still risks, but there is much greater medical confidence in dealing with them. There are risks in anything worth doing.

Some doctors put the risk of miscarriage and foetal deformity as high as three or four times the norm; others maintain that with good control there is virtually no extra risk at all. But babies born to diabetic mothers are often fat, puffed up with excess sugar and water and weighing in at nine pounds or more. And these babies, by a miserable twist of logic, can be born hypoglycaemic, as high blood sugar has passed through the mother's placenta to the foetus, causing it to supply extra insulin from its own pancreas to cope with the increase. Then, after birth, when the baby's blood glucose is no longer pushed up by the mother's, it nevertheless continues to produce a lot of insulin and unless given some sugar with its milk, the infant can become hypoglycaemic and risk brain damage.

Traditionally, diabetic mothers are given Caesareans to avoid the extreme stresses of childbirth, but there is a growing tendency – in keeping with the naturopathic school of birth – to deliver them normally. To some extent this is in response to mothers' wishes, but it is also a result of recent research which suggests that normal delivery squeezes the baby's lungs and helps clear them of fluid.

Childbirth is a controversial branch of diabetes and it is partly so because of the risk of parents passing diabetes on to their children. But how far diabetes is hereditary is a vexed question, to which no one can give a definite answer. There is certainly a hereditary element present but it is inconsistent and unpredictable.

A child with one insulin-dependent parent runs approximately a five per cent risk of becoming insulin-dependent himself and a child with one mildly diabetic parent runs approximately a twenty-two per cent risk of developing the same condition in later life. If both parents are insulin-dependent the child's risk goes up to ten or fifteen per cent and if both parents are mildly diabetic the risk goes up to approximately forty-four per cent.*

Sometimes diabetes descends through generation after generation, sometimes it skips a generation, and sometimes it affects people with no family history of diabetes at all. My mother's grandfather died of diabetes but that is a pretty remote link, and as far as I know there has never been a recurrence of the illness anywhere else in the family. Diabetes

*Identical twins inherit exactly the same genes from their parents. King's College Hospital in London tested 150 sets of identical twins and found that in only fifty per cent of cases were both twins diabetic.

often seems to run across rather than down families, affecting brothers, sisters and cousins, but in my family it has so far stopped at me. Luckily.

Research into the hereditary incidence is all rather inconclusive and, as far as I am concerned, unimportant. I would not hesitate to have children, even if every member of my family since creation had been a diabetic. Not just because I consider it, as serious diseases go, a second division one, but because I think it is always better to have life, however troubled, than not to have it.

In the last five years research has looked into the possibility that susceptibility to diabetes (rather than diabetes itself) is hereditary. Families with one insulin-dependent member are given blood tests to see whether the chemical defences of their white blood cells against infection contain over-active antibodies which destroy the pancreas's beta cells as well as the foreign virus cells that attack them. If it were possible to identify the over-active antibodies, which are a high diabetic risk, and to identify the infections they over-react to, it might be possible to immunise against over-reaction and so, in some measure at least, against diabetes. The second plank in this two-pronged attack would be regular exercise, weight-watching and control of carbohydrate in the diet. It makes sense in a tediously careful sort of way, but I do not like it. Immunisation – yes. But preventive living? And it is all for the sake of worry about something that might or might not happen, in a future that might or might not come. It's not how I would like to live.

High-risk antibodies look like being confirmed as hereditary but even if they are, they only have juvenile not adult diabetic potential. And it looks increasingly as if juvenile, insulin-dependent diabetes and adult, mild diabetes are clinically separate, though related, diseases. There is still a long way to go before anyone gets to the heart of the matter: namely, what causes diabetes?

6

A Strange Unquiet Wonder

The skies I travel under
A strange unquiet wonder.
(Patrick Kavanagh, *The Intangible*)

So far, no one knows what causes diabetes. There are myriad possibilities, indications, tendencies. The fashionable fad, current throughout the medical world at the moment, is to suggest that viruses may be responsible. A good proportion of current diabetic research is guided by the belief that diabetes, immune responses to infections, viral infections and hereditary cell composition are all interrelated. This theory was given a boost recently by a dramatic case which hit the headlines in America. A ten-year-old boy living near Washington got a flu-like infection which shot his blood sugar up so high that he was rushed to hospital in a keto-acidocic coma. He was given insulin but he did not respond and died a week later. A post mortem showed that a common virus, Coxsackie B4, had caused his diabetes and that, between them, the infection and the diabetes had killed him.

One of the possible conclusions researchers drew from this case was that viruses like Coxsackie B4 may do sub-clinical damage to the pancreas, which in turn predisposes its victims to diabetes. Further research has put twenty-six viruses, including glandular fever and mumps, on the diabetogenic (likely to cause diabetes) blacklist. Even coughs and colds are suspect. In 1972 a Midlands survey showed that the majority of juvenile diabetics developed diabetes between January and March, the peak time of year for coughs, colds and flu. The summer months saw far fewer cases.

A bad shock can trigger off diabetes – a car crash, accident, bereavement or an emotional crisis. As there did not seem to be any obvious reason for my diabetes, the doctors questioned me exhaustively about my life immediately before I started to develop symptoms: had I had a lover's quarrel, a family row, walked into a wall, lost a fortune? I could not help them. I had been happy and secure.

Nor does the over-eating and under-exercising – the biggest cause of adult diabetes – apply to cases of juvenile diabetes like mine. The two forms have similarities but their relationship to each other remains enigmatic, as do their causes.

Research into diabetes is concentrated on cause and treatment, and at present the emphasis is on treatment. In the last ten years a great deal of money has been put into diabetic research in America and Europe, in the hope that better treatment will reduce the incidence of heart disease, blindness and all the other troubles associated with diabetes. Research projects spring up all the time, and all manner of ideas and schemes are tried out. The most successful of these so far has been pancreas transplantation, pioneered at Cambridge. A new pancreas can save a severe diabetic from his condition and give him a new, non-diabetic life. Some patients are even given a new pancreas without the old one being removed so that if the transplanted organ fails to function they can easily fall back on the old one.

As with all organ transplants, rejection is a serious problem. It is especially so with diabetics because the steroids given to overcome the possibility of rejection raise blood sugar and thus worsen all the complications of the illness. However, a new anti-rejection drug called Cyclosporin A has been developed which only has to be used for short periods. It was this new drug which cleared the way for the first pancreas transplant in 1979.

A pancreas is a slimy thing. After transplantation it tends to leak digestive juices which destroy tissue and make it septic. But this particular difficulty was ingeniously overcome by an unlikely piece of Anglo-French co-operation. French doctors were the first to think of tandem transplants, leaving the old pancreas in place while implanting a new one, and they found a way of plugging the leaks in the transplanted organ with injections of synthetic liquid rubber. Unfortunately the synthetic rubber proved toxic and they could find no safe alternative. Then the Cambridge transplant team stepped in. Using the academic network, they got an old Cambridge man in the Malaysian Rubber Producers' Research Association to produce a natural rubber latex which could be used in the same way. It proved harmless to human tissue, and in August 1979 the first pancreatic transplant was done in Addenbrooke's Hospital, using the rubber to stop the new pancreas leaking.

The patient was a woman with end-stage kidney disease for whom a transplant was the last hope. She was given a new kidney and a new pancreas to work in tandem with her old one. Just over a month after the operation she was discharged from hospital, no longer diabetic.

In the year after that first transplant, ten more were done. Six were successful and the patients completely recovered and were cured of their diabetes, though it is still too early to say whether their recovery is permanent. Two operations failed but left their patients with their old pancreases; no worse off than they were before. Two of the patients died during the operation. But that is better arithmetic than dangerously severe diabetes offers when left to itself.

The Americans, too, have taken up transplants in a big way and I have no doubt that very soon it will be the exception to be severely diabetic and not be offered the possibility of a transplant. Unless, of course, something better comes along in the interim.

Currently, the other American enthusiasm is the pump or, as it is properly called, insulin infuser. The idea behind this device is that a continuous small infusion of insulin should prevent swings of blood sugar between high and low; the plague of the brittle diabetic's life. Instead of injecting large doses of insulin several times a day, you have a needle stuck in you all the time, attached to a pump which feeds the body with insulin at a fixed low rate all day and all night. American, Japanese and German pumps are small. They can be implanted in the body, like a pacemaker, and left there until the battery needs renewing while a micro-computer fixes the amount of insulin they infuse. However, English pumps – like the one I have used and can therefore describe – are not of that order. Not yet anyway.

When pumps were first talked of a few years ago, it occurred to me that the ideal must surely be a pump connected to a blood test stick. That way you could infuse as much insulin as the blood test told you was necessary. The other day a doctor who had been looking round Guy's Hospital's research unit told me that they had just got some pumps like the one I had imagined. He also said that the Japanese had invented a technique of continuous blood sugar monitoring and of connecting that to an infusion pump. It tells you and gives you exactly the amount of insulin you need, minute by minute.

It must be a mirage: it is, in effect, an artificial pancreas. Apparently there are technical problems and I bet it means a great hassle with needles stuck in all over the place. But what a mirage; a new life. I dare not even think about it.

I was fitted with a more traditional pump two years ago. It was a short, stormy and disastrous relationship, not at all the equable mean it should have been. But I can see that if it worked, and it does work for most people, it would be ideal. The model I was given was seven inches long and three and a half inches wide, comprising a plastic container with a battery and a motor to press home the plunger of the syringe, at a rate fixed by a dial on the side. There was also a button used to infuse more insulin before each meal. The syringe lay along the top of the container, held on by a rubber thread. I filled the syringe with insulin and tied it to the container before fitting a narrow plastic tube about two feet long over the mouth of the syringe. The insulin went through this tube and through the needle at the end of it into my stomach, thigh, arm or wherever I had inserted the needle for twenty-four hours. I had to make sure the tube was full of insulin before I put the needle in, otherwise I would have infused myself with air. I also had to stick the needle firmly in place with sticking plaster, to stop it working its way out.

My pump was big and unwieldy; not exactly what they call 'user friendly'. One press of the button pushed the syringe .23mm, so to push it 1mm you had to push the button four times. But insulin is measured in units and one unit is .7 of a mm so to inject one unit you had to press the button 4×.7 times. Every time you pressed the button it buzzed. So injecting ten units before dinner became a mortifying barrage of buzzes – and an exercise in concentration as the count went up to thirty or forty.

The pump also hampered mobility: it had to be firmly secured before any vigorous exercise like tennis or cricket. It also had to be removed before swimming or bathing, and I had to refill the syringe every twenty-four hours, with the result that the needle and sticking plaster combined to leave my stomach looking like a battlefield, with red patches, grey

103

plaster outlines and little septic holes. Another maddening consequence was that one-piece clothes nearly always had to have holes cut into them to accommodate such an infernally large machine.

But the main problem I had was with the syringe. It would work loose from its rubber fastening and fall back, pushing in the plunger and injecting all its forty units of insulin in one go. When the doctor gave me the pump he said I might find I was sugary for a while – a lot of people with continuous infusions were – but the one thing I could not be was hypo. However, I was continuously hypo for the next thirty-six hours. In the end we solved the slipping syringe problem with a rubber band, though I felt that my pump could have benefited from some more sophisticated modifications.

When it worked properly I felt sugary, as the doctor had warned me I would. I put the basal rate up, the injections up, the starch down, had little shots of insulin every two hours, and turned into a sugar-lump. I had not been so sugary since before I was diagnosed.

I am ashamed to say that when I left hospital three days after being fitted with the pump I wept. It was lovely to be going home and I packed in the twinkling of an eye. The nurse brought me all the things I would need for the pump: coils of tubing with needles and plastic butterflies, syringes, needles, boxes of sterile swabs, rolls of plaster, spirit to rub the plaster off, test sticks for blood tests, bottles of insulin. She piled all this on the end of my bed and to my horror I started crying. I am supposed to be a cheerful person and no one knew what to do with me. I squeezed all the stuff into a holdall and thanked the nurses, still sobbing. I went out to my bike with tears streaming down my face, piled everything into the basket, found I had lost the key to the padlock and carried on crying. I asked the porters for help and they sent me to see the clerk of works who sawed through the padlock, whistling. I thanked him and he said, 'That's all right, love. Things aren't that bad, are they?'

I agreed that they weren't and went on crying.

I cried all the way home and was asked to lunch by my sweet neighbours, who took no notice as I plopped tears on to the lettuce. I was so sugary that I could not stay awake and went to have a lie-down. I woke up two hours later, still crying. Then I made myself stop, though I went on feeling abysmally and inexplicably miserable for days.

The chief danger with pumps is that you can drift into being very slightly hypo without noticing, so that it carries on giving you insulin, making you more hypo, and the more hypo you are the less capable you become of doing anything about it.

Although I did not adjust to life on the pump, the idea is clearly an excellent one and research is improving design and efficiency all the time. Pump doctors at Guy's are currently assessing whether pumps help to prevent kidney trouble, and in Newcastle specialists are looking into the help they could give to the control of unstable diabetes.

Apparently about half the people who are given pumps cannot stand them: the other half love them. Men like them more than women; it makes them feel safe to have a machine in charge and they do not mind its ugly appearance so much. And even those who hate pumps admit that they do even out blood sugar. It did not hurt having the needle stuck in me all the time; I could hardly feel it. I put it sideways into my stomach because if I put it in vertically the needle hurt when I bent over. It was something I grew to live with, though never totally accept.

But the only time I ever felt free was when I took the pump off to have a bath. Otherwise it was with me night and day. The reward of pulling out the needle, scouring the sticking plaster marks with spirit, disconnecting and unthreading the

105

pump was a free – if wayward – body. I hated being chained to the pump; I could not even put on a dress without the rigmarole of disconnection, concealment and checking. Playing tennis, I had to lash the pump down and wait for it to fall off. It was impossible to be spontaneous and I came to see it as a perpetual constraint – a lesser beast. But in a way, now that I am back to my old, brittle and injecting self, and to that other beast, I look back to that month-long respite from hypos and see it as golden in retrospect.

More generally, technology is rampant in diabetic medicine. London's Charing Cross Hospital, for example, is developing computer-based teaching programmes for diabetics, in keeping with the modern trend for helping sufferers to help themselves. Across the river at St Thomas' Hospital they use computers for the comparatively humble task of storing records so information about patients can be easily assessed and used.

Ironically, the more computerised life gets, the more naturopathic; the higher the technology the higher the fibre. Diabetes is no exception. Oxford is the high fibre capital of the universe and doctors there do intensive studies on the effects of different diabetic diets, including the relative efficacies of diet and insulin. There are any number of studies on insulin, which is a consoling thought as I imagine that this means they must be researching into hypoglycaemia, too. The weight of insulin research seems inclined towards investigating diet and drugs as possible alternatives to insulin, or at least as supplements to lessen the amount of insulin a severely diabetic patient must depend upon. Doctors at King's College, London, and at the John Radcliffe in Oxford are currently studying the effects of insulin and diabetes on pregnancy and foetal malformation, whereas insulin and glucose function are the subject of studies in Dundee, Oxford, Glasgow, Manchester and Northwick Park. More technical studies of insulin action in cells – a fundamental area of diabetic medicine – are in progress in Oxford and in the universities of York, Leeds and Newcastle.

The universities of Southampton, Bath and Manchester have researchers studying the activity of insulin in fat cells and its relation to diabetic metabolism, while Sussex University is doing a research programme into the relationship between diabetes and liver activity. A number of studies of this sort conclude that the control of diabetes has an important effect on the complications that threaten, which is good news for those diabetics who are well controlled.

St Bartholomew's Hospital, London, the universities of Manchester and Glasgow, the London School of Ophthalmology and Hammersmith Hospital are studying kidney, heart and eye diseases in diabetic patients. It appears that diabetics are more prone to infections than other people and an Edinburgh doctor has shown that a surfeit of blood sugar can weaken the body's defence cells.

On the whole the emphasis in such academic research is on causes rather than treatment, though there is plenty of work being done on both. The genetics and hereditary behaviour of diabetes remain top priority but new techniques and new angles are being investigated all the time.

Surprisingly, diabetes varies from one country to another; not just the treatment, but the illness itself, which acts like a barometer of local diet, living conditions and geographical peculiarities.

There is an International Diabetes Federation based in England which collects information from all over the world and tries to deduce patterns of cause and effect. I wrote asking for help with this part of the book and they responded with a flood of articles, pamphlets and even a book about international diabetes. Much of the information was new to me, and provided unusual insights into particular societies as well as into their different types of diabetes.

For example, there are far fewer insulin-dependent diabetics in South-East Asia than there are in Europe and America, which must add support to the current European and American diabetic preference for a low fat, high carbohydrate and fibre diet; just the kind of diet eaten in South-East Asia. In Japan nearly all diabetics are treated with pills (including juvenile diabetics who would be given insulin elsewhere), for the extraordinary reason that it is illegal for patients in Japan to give their own injections. Many doctors ignore this law but some adhere to it and their insulin-dependent patients have to go to health centres every day to be given their injections by nurses. I am glad I am not Japanese. But I was impressed by Japanese politeness; the professor of diabetic medicine at Nishi-Shihbashi, Tokyo, wrote me a detailed letter about diabetes and its treatment in Japan, in reply to my request for information.

In all South-East Asian countries poor patients receive hospital treatment and medicines free of charge, a benefit which is sometimes extended to out-patient care, too. The rich use the flourishing private practices, but the so-called middle class fall between two stools and consequently have the hardest time.

South American countries are vast, the rural population is scattered and medical resources are hopelessly inadequate. Only about twenty per cent of the population qualify for free medical treatment. There is no overall system for teaching people to control their diabetes and the high rate of illiteracy means that each diabetic has to be personally taught to read his syringe markings with the aid of a coloured code, which has to be changed every time the dose is changed. I suppose that if a Peruvian Indian living hundreds of miles from the nearest hospital developed diabetes, he would simply die. However, one encouraging sign is the growing number of 'day centres' being built which help people to cope with their condition. The sooner diabetes everywhere stops being hospital-based, the better, but in developing countries – where hospitals and doctors can only treat a tiny percentage of the population – it is imperative.

In the Third World generally there are the obvious problems of poverty, illiteracy, shortage of money, facilities, doctors, nurses, teachers and dieticians. It is a long list of deprivation, and one which diabetes serves to heighten; Kenya, for example, has only two dieticians working in government hospitals. And there are ethnic and logistical problems, the biggest and most obvious one being that people who live in the teeth of starvation cannot be persuaded to limit their consumption of carbohydrate. If it is there, they eat it. They would be mad not to. It is only in wealthy societies like our own that we are able to eat a lot of fat and protein and can afford to be restrained about carbohydrate.

When I first went out to India I could not believe how much rice people ate and how thin they stayed. But I soon realised that it was because they ate hardly anything else; hardly any meat, fish, eggs, fat or vegetables; no cheese; very little sugar. They lived on rice and consumed it with the urgency of people who often did not have enough. In India, as in most developing countries, it is impossible to get people to diet. Diet is an indulgence of affluence, and in the Third World limiting carbohydrate consumption is suicide. Egyptians, for example, will not diet under any circumstances. Those doing well put on weight with triumphant delight as a sign of success and prosperity. In most of Africa the idea of diet is a bad joke.

I read an article in the 1980 issue of the International Diabetes Federation about diabetes in Ethiopia, in which the author explained the Ethiopian attitude to diet. It is totally uncomprehending. Weights, measurements and written recipes for cooking are unheard of. The staple food is *injera*, a sour pancake-like bread made of millet flour which is eaten

109

with *wat*, a vegetable stew made with starchy vegetables like pulses, or – in rich households – with meat, hotted up with pepper and spices. But most Ethiopian diabetics are poor and thin. They would not change their eating habits even if they could: fuel is expensive and poor families cook on a single charcoal brazier which makes a separate meal for one member of the family out of the question. And after the terrible 1984 famine the situation has, of course, become much worse.

Ethiopian Coptic Christians follow strict fasting laws during Lent, so the incidence of hypoglycaemia increases sharply just before Easter. The very devout eat absolutely nothing from dawn until after the midday Church service. I call that heroic: mad, but certainly heroic. I only fast two days a year, on Ash Wednesday and Good Friday, when I eat two very small meals and one ordinary meal which, by Ethiopian standards, is not a fast at all. But then I live a privileged life, in a privileged country. Many Ethiopian diabetics go undiagnosed, as do the majority of sufferers all over Africa. Many cannot get enough insulin or hypoglycaemic drugs, suffer ghastly side-effects and die. A lot of patients die in sugar comas because they just cannot afford the insulin they need. Tragically, there have even been cases of Ethiopian diabetics dying after changing from insulin to holy water. Only the very poor get free treatment, and only if they are able to get to a hospital. It all makes me feel spoilt. Articles about diabetes in developing countries are full of the kind of statistics about doctor/patient ratios and medical supplies that make me feel embarrassingly lucky.

Some of the articles I read described a phenomenon that was news to me: namely, the fact that the incidence of diabetes increases dramatically when people move from a rural to an urban life-style. No one seems to be sure why that is, but most of the people who have studied the phenomenon think it must be because of the unfamiliarity of urban life for traditional rural people, who move into a much more pressurised and less physically fit world. It is an alarming fact that bodes ill for countries like India where, although eighty per cent of the population still lives in villages, urbanisation is spreading apace.

India, in common with a number of developing countries, has a brand of insulin-dependent diabetes which is caused by malnutrition, the opposite extreme to the mild obesity-induced diabetes common in developed countries. It is known as J type pancreatic diabetes. It affects emaciated young people with a history of malnutrition which, presumably, has damaged their pancreases. There is a further refinement of J type, known as Z type, caused partly by malnutrition and partly by the consumption of cassava, which contains more cyanide than is good for you when eaten in large quantities. Cassava is the staple crop in Kerala, the only state in India where Z type diabetes is found. The third and final brand of letter-named pancreatic diabetes is K type, which is caused partly by malnutrition and partly by drinking a great deal of alcohol. Not surprisingly, its incidence is also more widespread.

Diabetes in the developed world is a different story altogether. Medical facilities and supplies are incomparably better; people are wealthier, more literate and more self-absorbed than they are in developing countries. They accept the value and vanity of dieting as part of their culture and have both the wherewithal and motivation to follow it through. But it is a cruel irony that the low fat, high fibre diet recommended all over the developed world today is in essence the diet of Third World countries, where people attest to their prosperity by expanding to higher fat, higher protein diets – the type of diet responsible for coronaries, strokes and bowel cancer in both diabetic and non-diabetic Western citizens. You cannot win.

111

But you can be grateful if you live, as I do, in Britain: not only is great care taken to teach me about the control of my illness, but I also get all my treatment and medicine free on the NHS. So does every diabetic in Britain, regardless of income and status. You do not have to go through the humiliation of getting a poverty certificate. You just fill in the exemption form on the back of the prescription and collect your insulin.

As I have already explained elsewhere, I prefer disposable non-NHS syringes which I have to pay for, but free ones are there for the taking, and they work. Being a diabetic in Britain need not be expensive. If you do not take insulin, you eat less and therefore spend less. If you do take insulin, you need plenty of bread and potatoes, which are cheap foods. There are jams, biscuits and chocolate manufactured specially for diabetics and these do tend to be dear but they are not essentials. I once bought a jar of diabetic jam which was delicious, exorbitantly costly, beautifully packaged, chic; primarily a work of art, only secondarily for eating. But one can survive with diabetes in Britain without being penalised; money provides additional luxuries, it is true, but the basics are free.

Most of western Europe gives its diabetics social security, insurance or National Health cover for the expenses of medicine and treatment. Eastern Europe has a similar system of organisation, with out-patients hospital clinics and local clinics treating patients, and insulin and drugs supplied free of charge or at very low cost. In Poland, for instance, insulin is supplied at ten per cent of its cost price, and when help for Poland was being asked for urgently a couple of years ago I took some bottles of old insulin to a collecting centre. They took it as if it were gold. I told them what strength it was but they did not seem interested; it was insulin and that was enough.

Being diabetic in America and Canada is alarmingly expensive; their health services are private and you have to find a company willing to insure you before you can recover any of your costs. Canada was the birthplace of insulin and now has a thriving diabetic association with plenty of group activity including diabetic holiday camps and self-help groups which are given great encouragement. Both America and Canada set great store by advanced technological research: Americans take artificial pancreases – pumps which give you insulin in response to continuous blood sugar tests – as a matter of course, but it will be a long time before they become so in Britain. Everything about diabetes in America and Canada smacks of money, technology and sophistication; a far cry from the still pitiful diabetic care available in the developing world today.

7

What Black Hours

What hours, O what black hours . . .
This night! what sights you, heart, saw, ways you went!
(Gerard Manley Hopkins,
I wake and feel the fell of dark, not day)

I hated the 1970s. That was when I got used to feeling
unhappy and ill. I lost the confident carelessness I used to
have, and I lost it because I was diabetic. I would have
preferred my loss to have been for a more exalted reason but
it was not. It was not because of any deep philosophical
disillusionment; not just because I was growing too old for
insouciance, though of course that was part of it; nor just
because of love, money, work or any of life's other important problems. The quality which A. A. Milne describes in
his Winnie the Pooh books as 'feeling all sunny and careless'
is the only one in my life I would definitely pick out as a
fatality of diabetes, and of diabetes alone.

Other things have taken its place which may well be more
valuable, but they are not the same; it is an irreplaceable
quality and, failing a miracle, an irredeemable one. As long as
I have to take insulin, I cannot imagine feeling that carelessness, that freedom to do nothing but live. It is not the
injections, nor the nuisance, soreness, swelling or paraphernalia that accompany each one – it is the menace of the insulin

114

itself. Insulin keeps me alive but it stalks my life like a hunter stalks its prey.

I remember reading *The Hound and the Falcon* by Antonia White, who used to go mad periodically. She called her madness 'the beast' and described how it overhung everything she did. Even when she was well and there were no problems, the beast was always behind her shoulder, waiting to attack. When everything was fine and everyone believed her to be free of her madness, she knew she was not, because she was always afraid of it coming back.

In the same way, I am always afraid of the insulin I take making me hypo. Not actively afraid, for I do not go around worrying about it, nor even thinking about it, but always at the back of my mind I am waiting for hypoglycaemia. And I wait for it with dread.

At first I was all right. I carried on as I had done before and when I went hypo I treated it as a one-off and forgot about it. I did various temporary jobs in London and when I got bored with that I went to France as an English teaching assistant for a term. By that time – the autumn of 1973 – I was feeling hypo quite often and it was while I was in France that I first began to get used to hypos, like you get used to the weather, and then to expect them, like you expect rain in November. I lived in a tiny room on the second floor of a prosperous provincial house with a grey slate roof and shuttered windows. My room was under the roof and had an iron bed that left space for nothing else except a table with a water jug and bowl. I lived like a minor character in a nineteenth-century Balzac novel. By the time November came, I had to break the ice in the water bowl in order to wash.

I did not feel anything like as well as I had felt before the onset of my diabetes but I could not say exactly *how* I felt ill. I was not in pain, I did not feel sick or dizzy or feverish; I just did not feel well. It was a new experience for me to be more than tired and more than miserable. I was mildly hypo all the time. I know that feeling now, as well as I used to know what it was like feeling well, and it is as impossible to describe. I taught lessons, picked fungi in the fields, walked round the allotments looking at the last gaudy dahlias and waited all the time for this feeling to get worse and send me really hypo. The doctors had told me to eat as little carbohydrate as possible so I could get by on as little insulin as possible and I took them too literally. I walked a starchless knife-edge and the few times I tried eating some bread or biscuits my blood sugar went up so high that I did not try it again. To compound the misery, I told everyone I felt all right because I almost did.

Despite all my protestations people said I was too thin. The big, boisterous family in the house on the corner of the square fed me gargantuan suppers with fat cheeses and good wines, but I never felt quite right. It's difficult to decide which were worse; the days when I felt obliquely ill all the time and slid down a slow slope into hypoglycaemia, or the days when I felt better, a born-again lover of life, only to lose my equilibrium and crash down between one moment and the next like a shot bird.

At half past ten one Saturday morning I remember looking at an old clock in the flea market, the sun clear and cold, the clock splendid in its shining brass. At ten thirty-one I was looking at the clock and not seeing it, my jersey wet with cold sweat, the stalls stretched horribly in front of me, the world became all mad and heavy. That morning the beast walked into my life. I have never shaken it off since, and I do not see how I ever will.

The feeling of nameless dread, the beast, is there every waking instant of my life and every night in my dreams, where it comes in the form of the frightful nightmares which hypoglycaemia induces. The faster I run to escape it, the faster it closes in on me, and its strength comes from my dread. I often feel quite well but, even when I do, I am poisoned with the dread of feeling hypo. If I walk to the shops feeling well, at the back of my mind I wonder how long it will be before I start feeling ill. If I defy the beast by playing tennis or going for a long walk – things I enjoy doing – the dread is the stronger that it will be spoilt the sooner. The more I do, the more I lay myself bare to the beast, and the more I have to lose.

So I do as much as I can. I would rather give the beast a run for his money than sit at home meekly, not using up much sugar in case I use up too much; if I do that, then I have surrendered the initiative. As long as I have spirit, I will go on doing as much as I want, even if it is often more than I can realistically do. At least I feel I have *earned* trouble that way. It is particularly dispiriting to sit sensibly with a book and feel the beast come nonetheless, soft-footed: first the fear – oh no, not again, not this time, it can't be – then the thing itself: dear God, get me out of this.

Three years ago I had the best holiday I have ever had with the people I love most in the world. That summer, the weather in the Scottish Highlands was perfect; a quick-change kaleidoscope of sun, storms and warm west-coast rain. The cottage was idyllic, perched above the sea looking across to the Hebrides. We ate the trout we caught in the lochs. I picked wild flowers and watched birds. It was para-dise and for two days I felt perfectly well. I felt as I had not felt for ten years; not a trace of sugar exhaustion, not the faintest hint of hypoglycaemia. I lay in the heather and could not believe how well I felt. That is how the beast lay down beside me, even in paradise.

I swam naked in the top loch, under a blinding, sunny sky, and knew it was on borrowed time. I picked the slender water lobelias out of the edge of the loch and took them down to the cottage. It rained one day but we fished anyway, then it cleared up abruptly and the sun came out on raindrops and cobwebs and wet stones. I walked beside a stream in a straw hat and thousands upon thousands of butterflies, hatched by the wet and the warmth, flew up around me in clouds. It was truly a glimpse of paradise and I lived it the more intensely because I knew it might end at any moment.

I lay in bed listening to the sea and thought that if I had only known in advance about the two glorious days ahead, I could have done something that I can never do except in heaven; I could have been careless. I could have escaped the beast.

It sounds overloaded, expressing it like that. Surely it cannot make so much difference, feeling well, especially as I often *do* feel well. But it does. I have no delusions about feeling well and feeling happy; happiness is not the difference I am trying to describe. It is simpler than that; it is the carelessness which I probably value too highly because I have lost it. I have become more aware of the loss over the years and, ironically, of the danger of making too much of it. There are worse troubles at sea and I have had an exceptionally lucky life. I do not resent the beast; but it is a release to write about it and articulate my fears, nevertheless.

The beast would not exist if hypoglycaemia were not so fearful. When I was in France I got my first intimation of its existence, but really no more than that as I had no idea then what a *bad* hypo could be like. But in the eleven years since then my hypos have got worse; sometimes in a slow progression and sometimes in leaps and bounds.

My hypos entered their dramatic stage when I came back from France and got a job teaching history at Cheltenham Ladies College. My sister says that when she was miserably unhappy in a job she was doing in London years later she used to say to herself, 'Tease stuck it at Cheltenham for two and a half years, so you can stick anything.'

118

I am the last person on earth who should have taught at Cheltenham Ladies College and I will never know why I did it, let alone how I stuck it for two and a half years. *Faute de mieux*, certainly.

I had an arts degree, could not type or take shorthand and refused to learn how to. But I was tired of bits-and-pieces jobs in London and wanted to use my brain. I liked teaching. I wanted to live in the country for a while. I was, and still am, uninterested in a career and I had a cheerful hope in the back of my mind, which I gradually lost, that I would get married and not have to bother much about jobs. Michael thought my being a Cheltenham lady was so funny that it could not be resisted. He took it as a sign that my spirit was driving on the wrong side of the road and was therefore obviously on the way to recovery. He drove me down to Cheltenham with the car stuck in top gear, laughing all the way.

I suppose it was funny, in a hellish sort of way. I survived by storing everything that happened in my memory and telling it to friends in London at the weekend, returning on Sunday nights for the next instalment. I lived at one remove from what I was doing and for a year or so my diabetes was similarly secondary. It dragged on me. I had to get permission from the headmistress to eat a sweet if I felt ill between lessons and once, during a staff meeting, I could feel sixty-five CLC mistresses nail me into disgrace with their stares because I ate a sandwich during a discussion about biros and pens. I was hypo too often to be above it all, despite the random telegrams that used to arrive from Michael instructing me to that effect. But it did not depress me. What it did do was make me watchful, and that is the mark of the beast.

The College knew from the beginning that I was diabetic, and for a year nothing happened that was serious enough to attract any attention. But then I did something which could not be ignored. I took my clothes off during a lesson.

I was taking quick-acting insulin twice a day and the

119

morning dose reached its peak action roughly an hour before lunch. Some days I would feel hypo by then and so would eat a sandwich with my coffee at break-time to give my sugar level a boost. One day I was teaching the last lesson before lunch when I began to feel peculiar. It was an 'O' level class and we were dredging our way through the rise of the Welfare State when I suddenly put my head down on the desk and left it there. The girls were not only well behaved; they were also the bottom set and not very bright. They just sat there looking vacant until I lifted my head. Then I started shaking it from side to side and repeating the same sentence over and over again; it was something about Keir Hardie and the trade union movement.

A few girls giggled nervously. I stood up and they stopped. I got up on my chair and they started again, while I proceeded to take off my pullover.

I remember it all graphically. I was wearing a black bra and thought, as I reached for the back to undo it, that I should have worn a white one; this one must have been showing through. Then the girl in the front row near the door suddenly jumped up and ran out of the room. She left the door open and a group of sixth form boys from Cheltenham College, who had some joint lessons with our school, stopped goggle-eyed in the corridor.

The girl came back with the history teacher from next door, followed by the school secretary with a cup of tea she was spilling all over the place. I knew I was being mad but I could not stop it. I watched myself drop my pullover and bra on to the floor, screamingly miserable and unable to do anything about it. I did not have a brain. I had a place in my head where my brain had been and where existence was being ground out of me by a mighty void. I got down quietly when they told me to and went and sat on a bench in the corridor, the secretary shooing the boys away and pouring sweet tea down my throat and bare neck. Someone wrapped my pullover round me and I sat silently, coming back inside myself. I am unusual – and unusually lucky – because I am not violent or aggressive when hypo. Instead I am without personality; a corpse performing a malignant parody of myself.

On this occasion I was back to my old self in a few minutes but had shocked the school enough to be given the afternoon off. I taught the same class the next day and they were wonderful: not a simper when I walked in minus my dignity. That is the nicest memory I have of Cheltenham.

Mercifully I have only stripped off diabetically on one other occasion and that was with a friend, thank goodness. If one must take one's clothes off out of context, a private audience is better than one comprising various startled members of Cheltenham Ladies College. But it is still not ideal.

A couple of summers ago, I went to a lunch party with a friend called Francis and stayed on talking to the hosts. I felt more and more removed and chatted less and less as the afternoon progressed. They asked me if I was all right and I said yes. But by the early evening I had clammed up completely and Francis took me out and called a taxi. He alleges that I stroked the taxi driver's arm. I am in no position to deny it but I do nevertheless, strenuously. We reached Francis' flat and he got me a drink of sugar and water, whereupon I took off my dress. As luck would have it, the day had been gloriously sunny and I was celebrating by not wearing any underwear. I sat down on the floor stark naked. I do not remember doing any of this but I am afraid it must be true because when I came back to myself a few minutes later I was still sitting on the floor, eating biscuits, and wearing nothing but a pair of earrings.

That is not all. Francis shared his flat with an Irishman who was living there until he joined a monastery. Before Francis had given me enough biscuits to pull me right round, I jumped up and said I wanted to go to the lavatory. That involved going past the kitchen, which I did, stark naked, just as the monk-to-be was coming out of it with a saucepan of steaming potatoes. Thank God for friends with a sense of humour. I was introduced to the monk-to-be more demurely when I was normal again a bit later and the three of us drank his Irish whiskey while I defended my thesis that hypoglycaemia only brings out your distorted nature, not your true one. It is the opposite to *in vino veritas*; the you that comes out in hypoglycaemia is not the real you at all, and that is one of the reasons it is so ghastly.

Michael was sympathetic about my hypos but did not really understand. There was no way he could have done and I think that men generally find it harder than women to believe in ailments which have no physical manifestation, as hypoglycaemia often does not. Illness for Michael meant a broken leg or scarlet fever; concrete afflictions. Anything invisible he was sorry for but in the end only believed up to a point. I did not have very bad hypos in the days when I knew Michael. I sometimes wonder whether it might have made a difference if I had. But it is water under the bridge now. Michael broke my heart during my last year in Cheltenham by marrying an Irish girl. It was not because she was in perfect health and I was not; it was because she was Irish and I was only half Irish, with an English accent to boot. And somewhere in the distance, unimportant but there all the same, was the fact that just now and then I was a tiny touch less extravagant in spirit than I had been during the earlier, halcyon days of our friendship.

After Michael left, I began to wonder about the potential diabetes had for ambushing my life, though it is a trap to blame it for things; you invariably end up regretting everything bitterly – and uselessly. But undoubtedly the beast stalked closer. Taking my clothes off had brought it nearer, as did the morning a few weeks later when I woke up to find that I could not move my left side.

At first I lay still for a few minutes, thinking I was still half asleep. But then I tried to get up and could not. My right side moved but when I tried to move my left it flopped and jerked like a puppet. It was not paralysed in the sense of being locked immobile, but it had no power. I could not lift my arm or my leg and when I tried to lift them with my right hand they fell straight back on to the bed, dead weights. I tried to roll to the right, hoping my weight would carry me on to the floor, but I did not have the strength. I lay back on the pillow and tried to collect myself. I was not afraid, just curious, and after another half hour of futile attempts to rub, bang and scratch my left side into activity, I decided to call for help.

My landlady lived on the floor below. It was very early in the morning, about five o'clock, but I did not know that because I could not see my watch properly; my eyesight was blurred. I started to shout but found, to my further surprise, that I could not speak properly either. My speech was slurred and all I could manage was a terrible sort of werewolf howl which woke Mrs Hart and brought her, astonished, into the room. I could not have told her what was the matter even if I had known, but I managed a nod when she asked if she should call a doctor. She sat with me until he came, asking me all sorts of comforting little questions like, 'Do you think it was something you ate?'

It was an inexpressible relief when the doctor arrived. I have had a lot of paralytic hypos since that one, most of them much worse, and each time I have felt the same surge of relief when someone – anyone – comes. After hours of being trapped in a writhing hypo, the sound of a door opening or footsteps approaching is a whisper from heaven.

In this case, though, the doctor happened to be the only one I have ever come across who was not an angel. In fact, had I not exhausted the word already, I would say he was a beast. He was young and neat and came straight up and said,

123

'This is hysterical. Stop it.' I looked at him beseechingly. The pillow and sheets were saturated with sweat and strands of hair stuck across my forehead and eyes. I tried to toss them out and others stuck in their place. The doctor told me to squeeze his hand with my right hand, which I did, and with my left hand, which I could not. I could not even lift it off the bed.

'I can't,' I said, the best I could, feeling suddenly desperately tired.

'You can,' he said. 'Come on, squeeze it.'

'I can't,' I said and laid my face on the damp pillow and wept. I cried because I was helpless. My only hope lay with this doctor and he did not understand. He said he knew I was diabetic; Mrs Hart had told him, but that could not be anything to do with my present trouble, which was hysterical; it was up to me to stop it, or he would give me a sedative.

I could see it getting light through the curtains and I felt utterly, utterly miserable. I did not think about being paralysed for life or anything like that, but I thought about what he had said and it hurt. I did not know what was wrong but I felt ill through every fibre of my being and the doctor offered no prospect of help. I looked up at him and his outline was watery with tears. His diagnosis notwithstanding, he went to fetch a glass of sugary water and put his hand under my head to help me drink it. I felt ashamed of my sweaty neck next to his immaculate sleeve.

As soon as I had swallowed the drink I felt better. The toes of my left foot wiggled when I moved them, then I moved my left leg and arm. I closed my eyes and did not care about the doctor. I lay still, not listening to what he was saying, not caring, not thinking anything except, 'I am alive; thank God.'

Something happens while I am in a hypo which is different from being alive, and when I come out of one, for a short time I am more than alive. After bad hypos I feel suffused with life. I can move again; I can think again; I am a person again. I treasure those times. Sometimes they only last for a few minutes, sometimes an hour or more. I do not want to talk to friends, listen to beautiful music, rest or celebrate. It is enough just to sit wherever I am and wallow in living.

Physically it is different. I am tough and can bounce back quickly but I do feel wrung out: peaceful but too tired to move. One day during that paradisial summer which I spent in Scotland I had a hypo which sent me into a coma for hours. My friends threw me into the back of their car and drove me round the hairpin Highland bends with tyres screeching, to the doctor. I am sorry to have missed it. The doctor gave me some glucagon and I woke up. We drove back and I lay on the back seat looking out at the mountains and the sea. They had never looked so beautiful. We got back to the cottage in time for breakfast and I drank a mug of coffee watching the mountain across the bay veiling and unveiling itself in the early morning mist. I remember that moment as feeling more than alive.

The sensation stayed with me all morning and pushed away the exhaustion. I walked with Guth, one of the friends, round the nearest loch and climbed the slope beside it, hanging on to rocks and birch trees on the way up. We reached the top and looked down at the paradise spread below us. Two hours before I had almost been dead.

Hypoglycaemia is a place you go to, and when you come back, then the place you physically inhabit at that moment of return is transfigured along with everything else. A mountain-top, a chair at home, a hospital bed; it does not matter which – it is blessed, just as the hypoglycaemic place is accursed. Every mental hypo I have had has involved going out of life into that place. It is black; a place lower than hell; a place too bad to exist until you go there. And I have visited it often.

Curiously, the time I experienced this most vividly was when I was, actually and physically, in the wrong place and the most horrific part of the hypo was coming out of it and returning to a place I could not recognise.

I had made a radio programme at Broadcasting House in London, after which I had snatched a quick supper with my producer in the cafeteria. There were long queues for food and drink and I had no time to go back and queue again when supper turned out to be less starchy than I had expected. The canteen had run out of potatoes and I took a bread roll instead, hoping it would be enough. After supper I took the tube to Paddington and got on the 9.45 train home to Oxford. The last thing I remember is the ticket collector saying, 'Don't forget to change at Didcot.'

The next thing I knew, I was walking round a strange town, looking for something familiar, but finding nothing. It was a big place, and almost empty of people. Then I turned a corner to see a station with BRISTOL TEMPLE MEADS over the front and a clock saying one-thirty.

I looked at the notice and started coming out of my hypo. It was a lightening, infernal journey: I must have slipped into a coma on the train, forgotten to change at Didcot and travelled on to the end of the line. They told me later it is called a 'white-out'; you go around seemingly normal with your brain in abeyance, on automatic pilot. I tried not to think about the four hours I had lost. What had I done since I got off the train? God knows; maybe part of Bristol does, but I never will.

I walked up to the station and told the man at the ticket barrier that I was diabetic and had come to Bristol by mistake. He looked sceptical and asked me what I wanted to do about it.

I said, 'I want to have a bun.'

He nodded an 'I thought so' nod.

'You want to have a bun,' he said.

126

'Yes please. I've got to have one.'

'You've got to have one.'

'Yes. If I don't have one I might collapse.'

'If you don't have a bun you might collapse.'

We could have gone on like that for hours, but fortunately another railwayman came over and asked what the trouble was.

'She's drunk.'

'I'm diabetic,' we chorused. The man was a dream. He took my arm and tucked it firmly under his and walked me through an underpass to a platform where he opened the door of an office. I went in. There was a coal fire, a table covered with newspapers open on the racing page, packets of tea and biscuits, and railway maps and timetables round the walls.

'Now you just sit there, honeysuckle,' he said, and I did so. Blissfully.

'I know all about diabetes. I'm a first aid expert.'

He made me a mug of the sweetest tea I have ever tasted and gave me a doughnut out of his tuck box. Usually you feel so ill when you are given sweet food that you do not enjoy it, but this time the tea made me feel better and I ate the doughnut in paroxysms of rapture. I told the railwayman he was fantastic and we went through the next day's racing cards together and he showed me railway maps from the fifties, sixties and seventies: almost as great a pleasure to look through as old *Wisdens*. I had met a wonderful man and it had almost been worth going to that place to do it.

At four-thirty a.m. he gave me a ticket for Oxford free of charge and put me on the mail train for Reading, waving goodbye with his cap. I was weary by then and lay on the seat, going over and over in my mind what had happened, or what I thought must have happened while the train stopped at every station. When we got to Reading I had an hour to wait for the Oxford train. It was still only about six-thirty a.m.

127

and I went into the Heathrow coach waiting room, the only warm place on the platform. It was deserted. I had just sat down when a young railwayman came in and told me to get out; the lounge was for Heathrow passengers only. There were none inside but I could see from his face there was no point arguing so I left and walked up and down outside, stamping my feet to stop them from going numb with cold. I had some BBC scrap paper in my handbag and sat and wrote a thank-you note to the man at Bristol, inspired to even warmer gratitude by the sight of the young railwayman sitting in the Heathrow lounge with his feet on a chair, smoking a cigarette.

I got home some nine hours behind schedule.

The doctors assure me that during a white-out one only does things that are in character. If one is normally pacific, one is not likely to commit murder. But, these reassurances apart, behaving in character is no comforting thought when your character is somehow warped: for all I know I may have stripped in a Bristol street on automatic pilot.

Some hypos are mainly physical, some are mainly mental and some are both. They share a common core of ghastliness but the ones I hate most are the mental ones. In the days when I was teaching in Cheltenham I did not get hypos like that. In fact, looking back to those early years and comparing them to the present, it was a piece of cake. But it was ghastly all the same.

I prefer physical hypos because they are only physically ghastly. The ones where I get paralysed do not get right inside me like the mental ones. They also tend to impinge more directly on other people and this is one of the unlooked-for blessings diabetes has given me; friends and strangers alike have invariably been kind to me over physical hypos, with the possible exception of that Cheltenham doctor (though in his defence one should plead Cheltenham, ignorance and early morning). Mental hypos, however, are a different proposition altogether. People are more alarmed by mental hypos and less good at coping.

I left Cheltenham Ladies College after two and a half years and went to Cambridge to do some research into medieval history. I was one of twelve graduate women accepted by Trinity College in 1976, before they opened the flood-gates to female undergraduates a few years later.

There happened to be a retired dean living just outside Cambridge who had done a lot of work on the medieval monastery at Ely and its estates, the subject of my thesis. He was kind enough not to object to my muscling in on his life's work; more than that, he was glad to help me with it. I used to go there for tea and sit by the fire eating crumpets from under a silver lid. He and his wife were well into their eighties, straight out of Trollope, absolutely delightful and absolutely proper. When I had known them a few weeks, they asked me to a party for which we made vol-au-vents, cheese straws and canapés to go with the drinks. It is harder to measure carbohydrates with that kind of food and I lost count when I became engrossed in a long, riveting story being told me by my elderly friend's nonagenarian brother-in-law about an occasion after the First World War when he had smuggled a woman into Russia in the diplomatic bag. I did not know how many carbohydrates I had already consumed so I ate a few more asparagus rolls to be safe. As with life, so with diabetes – better to overdo it. But as luck would have it on this occasion, I underdid it.

I was to spend the night in the nearby manor house with the elderly foreign office man and his wife. My bedroom was splendid and high-ceilinged, lovely to sleep in but a long way from the rest of the house and the other inhabitants. If your blood sugar drops, as mine does, during the night, you do not know about it because you are asleep. If it drops into hypoglycaemia, you sometimes wake up shivering and

129

sweating and can go and get some sugar. I always keep some Dextrose tablets beside me for just this sort of emergency. But sometimes it goes on dropping without waking you and that is what happens to me most of the time. It reaches its lowest point at about four in the morning and I either go into a coma or wake up paralysed.

That morning I woke up and found that I could not do anything. I was paralysed from the neck downwards on both sides. I willed myself to move, ferociously. I could see my Dextrose tablets where they lay beside the pillow, but I could not get at them. I tried and tried and could not do it. I was miserably conscious of having soaked the lovely linen on the bed with sweat – which stupidly made me reluctant to call for help. I lay hoping that the paralysis might wear off but knowing it would not because I had taken slow as well as quick-acting insulin the evening before and it would last for hours more.

So, apologetically, I started to scream. The lady I was staying with was younger than her husband – only about seventy-five – but even so, and even after life in a diplomatic *Boys' Own* environment, a screaming, incoherent paralytic before breakfast was a touch *de trop*, I felt. I screamed in an experimental sort of way for about five minutes and when that failed to produce any action, I screamed with more commitment for another five minutes. Nothing. I was at one end of the house. They were at the other end, partially deaf and tired after the party.

I could not even move enough to make myself fall out of bed in the hope that the crash would wake them up. I could not wipe the sweat out of my eyes. There was nothing, simply nothing, I could do, except scream. So I did. I lay screaming, then lay quiet from exhaustion – alternately – for three hours.

It was a long three hours. I told myself it would pass in the end and I prayed for help. Not for the paralysis to go; I knew it would not, but for unspecified help: peace, calm, strength, someone to hear me; whatever God felt like giving me. But He just gave me what He usually does; nothing perceptible except continued existence.

At seven-thirty I heard a door open at the other end of the landing and slippered feet scuffing along towards me. Moments later I saw the lady I had been so longing to see, in an old camel hair dressing-gown, her grey hair hanging loose. Paralysed and one-sided it may have been, but I gave her a smile containing three hours of heart-felt gratitude. This lady did not turn a hair. She saw the Dextrose tablets and asked me if they were what I wanted. I nodded. Sustained as ever by a sense of occasion, she disappeared and came back a few minutes later with a pot of tea and two exquisite china cups and saucers. She sat on the edge of the bed and poured two cups of tea, putting Dextrose tablets into them both and tipping mine into my mouth as if it was something she did every day. As soon as I could speak I said thank you.

'Not at all, my dear. I always have early morning tea and it is so much nicer sweet.'

Then with a linen napkin she mopped up tea that had spilt on to the pillow and asked me what I thought she should do about the buddleia in the shrubbery; it was showing signs of strain.

It has been like that time and time again. People are marvellous. The help they give, however frenzied or inefficient, has always saved me in the end. I have one close friend who has helped me through innumerable hypos, from the sullen to the comatose, and he is the only person I talk to in any depth about what I feel like. It is impossible to explain, but trying makes a special kind of intimacy. One person like that is enough; one person to understand, if not the beast itself, then the power of the beast in my life.

This friend, James, is healthy to the point of hyper-activity, which makes his understanding all the more remarkable. James is patient about tiredness and, when it comes to hypos, he is dynamic. I remember him once pouring sugary milk down my throat with a funnel, the sort you use to put petrol in cars, because he could not get me to swallow it any other way.

I was once staying overnight in his spare room when he came in and could not wake me up in the morning. He tried sugary milk, bread and honey, and Dextrose tablets. I must have been in quite a deep coma because even the Dextrose had no effect. All that happened when he held them against the inside of my cheek was that they fizzled out between my teeth. He called an ambulance which arrived – as ambulances have always arrived in my experience – in less than five minutes. James' flat is right at the top of a narrow London house and the ambulancemen had to carry me in a canvas stretcher-chair down one flight of stairs after the next, turning murderously sharp corners, though I do not remember anything about it.

The first thing I do remember is waking up in hospital with a needle stuck in a vein and a doctor talking about ccs and milligrams. I did not know where I was but it did not take me long to work out that it was a hospital. How and why I had got there were another matter. The doctor asked me if I had missed dinner last night after taking my insulin but I had not; I must have suffered one of those random falls in blood sugar that happens inexplicably once in a while.

It was, as is usual with me, five-thirty in the morning. I apologised for being a nuisance and he said it did not matter; my hypo had given him practice doing intravenous injections. I looked at my arms which were peppered with bruises and blood spots, as was the back of my hand, which was blue-black, and even my foot, where he had finally found a susceptible vein. I answered his questions about my diabetes

132

and who looked after it. Then he asked me if I often had hypos like that. I asked him what he meant by often, and when he said twice a year, I smiled again. Today, at the time of writing, I am, miraculously, in remission; I have hardly had any early morning hypos for months, but until this year I was having them every few weeks. I thought of the woman I had sat next to at an out-patients clinic who told me about her dreadfully unstable diabetes. She had once, she said, had such a bad hypo she had to go to hospital. I felt effortlessly and sadly superior.

The doctor left and I looked round at my surroundings. I was in one of the individual, curtained cubicles that make up every casualty department. They are all the same, each having shelves of needles, syringes, tubes and sinister contraptions in plastic bags. There is always the same light on the ceiling: flat and round, with a mauvish white bulb. I feel at home in casualty departments now and lie happily contemplating their familiar adornments.

If I am lucky and they have forgotten to draw the curtain, I watch the doctors and nurses go by outside and the patients being wheeled, carried, pushed and trundled. The sound effects are the grimmest part. I have heard people puking gallons, spitting out teeth, gurgling, groaning, screaming, moaning, breathing avalanches of rocks in and out and pouring rivers of blood. Eavesdropping on nurses discussing doctors' mistakes is light relief by comparison.

This time the curtain was open and I sat up to see James coming towards me. He had followed the ambulance in his car. I hate to think what I must have looked like – pasty and dishevelled – but whatever my appearance, he looked worse: half dressed, unshaven, pale and exhausted. He said they had taken a long time trying to get me round and he had sat on a bench to wait. There had been nothing to do except flick through an old copy of *The Economist*, which he had read twice then put under his head, intending to get some sleep. He had been woken up by a cleaner who poked a broom at him and said, 'We can't have types like you coming in here to sleep. Out you go. Go round to the Salvation Army and ask them for a cup of tea.'

The cleaner had made him pick up the paper holdall into which he had thrown my clothes – he thought it was a vagrant's sandwich bag – and hassled him away. Poor James. I felt radiantly well, as always after hypos, but upset to have caused so much trouble. When the nurse brought me some sweet tea and biscuits I gave them to James, who needed them more than I did. Then we thanked everyone and left.

James drove off at a great pace, fed up with the hospital, and before we had gone quarter of a mile a police car forced us into the side of the road. There were all the usual questions about speeding which I knew by heart from my days with Michael (who never let the cops catch him without a chase). James' tactics were different and rather good. Instead of saying, as Michael used to, that the car was stuck in top gear or that he had not noticed the speed limit because he was looking up to heaven and saying a prayer, James simply told them that he was driving me home from hospital.

The policeman looked at me suspiciously whereupon I showed him my bruises and plasters. I leant my head back against the seat and smiled faintly. They let us off with a caution and we drove back to James' flat, amused that the police had forgotten to ask us the vital question; why we were in such a hurry driving away from the hospital, and not towards it.

8

Sugar Plumbs

And eating haws like sugar plumbs ere they had lost the may . . .
(John Clare, *Remembrances*)

I could write a hypoglycaemic guide to hospitals all over the country, from Inverness to Cheltenham, and I would give them all high marks. I could not do anything else; they have saved my life. But obviously some are better than others and, in my opinion, the smaller the better. When I was living and working in Cheltenham I attended out-patients clinics at the Westminster Hospital in London about twice a year. It was so impersonal; I saw a different doctor every time, told him I was all right and went away again. When I moved to Cambridge I went to Addenbrooke's, a vast pile with a tall chimney that makes it look like a crematorium. By then I had to go to clinics more often, about once every two months, because the doctor I saw there did not think much of my diabetic control. (He was right: my blood sugar went up and down like a lift.) Then, while at Cambridge, I had my first hypoglycaemic coma and soon I had to go to clinics once a month.

Wherever the hospital, and however friendly, there is always a thing called a waiting area where wheelchairs, white sticks and *Good Housekeeping* magazines (usually *circa* 1969, and minus recipes) abound. Clinics make most people tetchy

135

and nervous but I do not mind waiting. I am lucky. I read a book or meditate, keeping everyone's symptoms, missed buses and matchlessly troublesome diabetes the other side of a protective silence. I smile and chat but only in short bursts. Once the conversation looks like getting serious, I drift off into silence.

The clinics at Addenbrooke's were the slowest I have ever known. I count on waiting at least an hour at any hospital but there I often found myself waiting two or three. Once I arrived at nine-thirty for an early appointment and had a blood test which showed a high blood sugar. I sat down and waited dutifully. People who arrived long after me came and went. After two hours I asked the receptionist whether my notes had perhaps got mislaid. The suggestion was received with horror, and I returned dutifully to my seat. The clinic emptied. In the end there was no one left but me. My notes had, of course, been lost and by the time they found them at twelve forty-five, my blood sugar had dropped through the floor. I went into the doctor feeling hypo and so unable to answer his questions coherently. He said my blood sugar was high and I had better take more insulin so in my hypo state I agreed, and drove home on my motor-bike like an hallucinating Italian.

I took more insulin as the doctor had advised because my sugar was too high in the early mornings, and ate more starch to balance it off. After a few days on this regime I woke up paralysed and screamed until the couple in the flat above me came down. He was a Greek and she a Scot; they pooled their temperaments, poured honey all over the bed and called an ambulance. I was taken to casualty and pumped full of glucose after which they said I could go home. It was then I realised that I did not have any clothes on. It was summer and I had been sleeping naked. Ambulancemen are not allowed to handle naked patients and they had covered me in my counterpane, in which I now wrapped myself and sat in my cubicle, an apparition in pink. The nurse said they had called a taxi to take me home.

I said, in my best bourgeois manner, 'But I haven't got any clothes on.'

'Oh dear, well never mind. We'll find you something,' she said and to my astonishment came back a few minutes later with a pair of blue plastic bags in her hand. Apparently it is against the law for a hospital to send you out with bare feet – though whether the rest of you is clothed doesn't matter – so the nurse had decided to give me a pair of the transparent covers surgeons put over their shoes during operations. I slipped them on, thanked everyone and went out to the taxi wearing the counterpane like a toga and the plastic bags like space shoes. When we reached the flat I did not have my keys and again had to wake the people upstairs before I could get in, find my purse and pay the taxi driver. George the Greek was aghast at the plastic bags and stomped upstairs muttering darkly.

The taxi driver looked amused as I gave him a huge tip and apologised for my garb.

He said, 'Darling, I've been driving a taxi in Cambridge for twenty years and this is the best fare I've ever had. First I get Lady Godiva, then she gives me a dollop too much money. There's not enough of it about.' He stuck his head out of the window as he drove away and yelled, 'And best of all, there's a hole in your blanket!'

One of the side-effects of hypos is that they make you fat. For the first three years of my diabetes I was extremely skinny; so thin that Michael told me I looked like a plank. I liked being thin but not that thin. My bosom had shrunk to nothing, size ten clothes were much too big and I had no energy. Sometimes just walking upstairs made me so tired that I had to stop half-way and have a rest. I still did not have

137

periods and I felt underdone all round, like a slice of meat, bloodless and uncooked.

But things began to change when I started to take more insulin. The doctor at Cambridge said it would be good for me to put on weight; I was only so thin because I was too sugary and the extra insulin would be good for me. But while my blood sugar went up and down my weight went up and up. Hypos make you heavy. I do not know why. They just do. It is not just the glucose they pump into you; it is the thing itself. One of the ways they can tell if you have been hypoglycaemic is to weigh you; if your weight has gone up and your blood sugar down, you have been hypo. I have never expected life to be fair, but this was worse than the days when I had eaten more, weighed less and felt too tired to live.

At Cambridge I did a great deal of my work in the manuscripts room of the University Library. Two hours at a time is enough to spend poring over the fourteenth-century scraps of tea-coloured parchment (covered in coffee-coloured hieroglyphics) which I was trying to piece together into a history, so I used to go down into the tea-room for a chat and a bite to eat whenever friends asked me. The tea-room was famous for its scones. There were cheese scones and sweet scones and I ate a cheese scone each morning at coffee break, still warm, with the butter running out of it. Everyone wolfed them gleefully. I liked them, though never as much as everyone else because I was not eating them through choice. It is the same with all eating. I like it, and I like cooking, with all the hospitality and sociability that meal-times entail. But food is never quite as it used to be: it now has this element of constraint about it.

Unlike most diabetics, I do not miss the food I have had to give up. Just now and then I get a sudden craving – at Christmas for Christmas pudding; after swimming in the sea, for chocolate; at random, for steamed golden pudding and golden syrup. I once dreamt about white chocolate like other people dream about sex. But mostly I do not mind. Having to eat when I do not want to is far worse. I know that when 11.00 a.m. approaches I have to eat some starch whether I'm hungry or not. Likewise I have to eat again at four in the afternoon, in addition to daily breakfast, lunch and supper. It is the compulsion and the routine I hate; gone are the days when I chased about and starved for three days then ate, drank and slept for the next three.

When my periods had come back and I had passed the recommended weight for my height, the doctor at Cambridge declared, 'Kindly stop gaining.' Then he added, 'See the dietician on your way out.'

Diabetes is designed for people with routine lives and if your diet is not constant from day to day, if you hesitate in recounting whether you eat a banana or two biscuits at coffee time, there is consternation. As for what time you have supper, variations like mine between 7.00 p.m. and midnight are regarded as close to psychotic.

The dietician's revenge is two-fold: carbohydrate and calories. Long, swingeing lists of them in all their horror and horrid, inescapable relationships. I know all the figures by heart and usually I throw my diet sheet away as soon as I can escape. If any of what I believe turns out to be true, I will pick up a diet sheet on the way to heaven, if I go that way, and eat it. In a white sliced bread sandwich with my mother's blackcurrant jam.

Nowadays, with the world gone metric, they weigh you in kilos which is, as my father would say, 'less worse' than stones and pounds. It is not quite so familiar, but soon develops its own particular barriers; ten stone used to be my horror mark beyond which I would not pass without recourse to starvation dieting; at present it is sixty kilos. And now I have almost passed even that. Oh, what a business! That it should ever enter one's head!

But I can't get away from it. Being weighed is the first thing you have to do at a diabetic clinic. You queue up in a line of other diabetics, the odd one skeletonous, the others mostly overweight. You hand a urine specimen across the counter for a girl to test for sugar. Then you climb on the scales and wait while they slide weights up and down the arm of the scales until it clangs down like the guillotine and they proclaim your weight *maxima voce* to the assembled multitude.

People's innocent comments can be unbearably hurtful. I went to a dinner party while at Cambridge where the hostess was on a diet and had planned a menu with as little carbohydrate as possible. I did not know that. All I knew was that I had just had my insulin injection and there was consommé with thin curls of toast instead of bread, parma ham without melon and sole with only a spoonful of sauce. I did not like to ask for a piece of bread because I did not know the hostess well and it might have seemed insulting to her cooking. So instead I began eating sliver after sliver of French toast, to the amazement of the other guests, who nibbled gracefully at theirs and passed me the whole basketful so they could watch me eat it all. I felt ill and remote. A piece of chicken arrived in front of me. Then suddenly there were potatoes; a steaming mountain of the blessed things right under my nose, with parsley sprinkled on top. I did not wait for anyone else. I stuck my fork straight in and put six on my plate. I could hear everyone go quiet and as I had shown myself ill-mannered and greedy already, I carried on regardless, scooping up and swallowing mouthfuls of potato in ecstasies of relief before anyone else had so much as got them on their plate. Then the man next to me said, 'Do you always eat this much? I should have thought you ought to be watching your figure.' I can still hear him saying it.

I remember another occasion at Cambridge when I ate

more than anyone else but in an altogether different mood and with happy results. It was when I played cricket for the University against Oxford – a game ideal for diabetics. It has action, contemplation and even breaks for eating.

I used to play for Cheltenham Women and when I went up to Cambridge I switched to the University Women's team. As it happened, I was the first woman to get a blue both for Oxford and for Cambridge, which is a lightweight achievement; the standard was low. But I regard even the smallest cricket honour as priceless and I am thrilled with mine. The first year I played for Cambridge the varsity match was away and we went across to Oxford in a coach. We stopped at a pub near the Wadham College ground we had booked to use and had a sandwich lunch. When we had had two sandwiches each there was one left over: someone offered the plate round and I took the sandwich, to be sure I had enough carbohydrate.

We lost the toss and fielded first. I had played irregularly during the season and could not understand why they had picked me for the match. I was a fast fielder and could bowl, but erratically; sometimes I spun the ball and snapped up wickets; other times I was prosaic and expensive. I always seemed to bowl better when it was sunny and the day of the varsity it was hazy with bursts of sultry sun. Our opening bowlers plugged away without success, the score ticked up and the Oxford openers looked demoralisingly professional.

'Wait now,' they called. 'Come on.'

After an hour the captain gave me the ball, telling me to be careful and remember that it was an important match. I set a serious field, with five slips and two gullies. I did not have the slightest idea what I was doing but I thought it crucial to make the enemy think I had. I tossed the ball from hand to hand and looked subtle. I bowled round the wicket, in case I could make it slope off across the batsman and into the slips. I did, but slowly, and the over cost eight runs.

141

For the next over I decided to crowd the bat and called up a short leg, leaving only one fielder in the deep, which cost another eight runs. Our captain looked peeved but she gave me the ball for a third over and told me it was my last. I bowled one ball round the wicket and then one ball over the wicket, confusing fielders, umpires and batsman alike and knocking the off stump quietly backwards like a retired colonel. Everyone was amazed. The umpire turned to me and said, 'A rare beauty. Came on with the arm and doubled back.'

I was too overcome to speak. I just smiled. The number three batsman came in and I got her lbw with my next ball. The sun came out and my happiness knew no bounds. To me, cricket is the only sport in which the joys are both simple and profound and mine that afternoon approached the sublime. I took eight wickets for forty-five runs in fifteen overs and four balls; it would have been for fewer runs if I had not got carried away and tried to bowl the last two overs fast with three silly mid offs.

When we stopped for tea our team made me blush with their congratulations. We sat on the pavilion steps in the sun and someone said, 'It must have been the extra sandwich. I knew there must be some secret reason.'

It came to me then, out of a glorious oblivion, that I had forgotten about my diabetes. I had not thought about it once. I do not know where the magic came from, and it has never returned. But that afternoon I played cricket like a dervish and although we eventually lost the match the beast had gone away.

The other activity I loved at university and, like cricket, still enjoy (though I do not do nearly enough of it) is dancing. Martin and I had danced our way through my last two years at Oxford, and after that I just took the opportunity whenever it turned up. Cheltenham was deadly so I was determined to make up for lost time when I got to Cambridge.

The senior tutor at Trinity was in charge of graduate students and interpreted his charge as being primarily one of entertainment. He was exuberantly energetic – despite a metal leg which was the result of a horrific car crash – and so were his dances. They burned up blood sugar at a prodigious rate. I ate three mince pies, normally a forbidden food, at one of his Christmas parties and used up their carbohydrate gyrating joyfully round the floor. We outlasted the fitness brigade and the rowing teams. Then, staggering back across Great Court afterwards, it somehow came up in conversation that I was diabetic. He asked me about it: did I have to have injections? How many? What were the best needles? How much did they cost? I answered politely and thought nothing more of it. But the next day I found a cheque for £50 in my pigeon-hole together with a note from the senior tutor saying that it came from a bursary fund for medical aid which they had been trying to spend for years but could not, because everyone in Trinity was too healthy.

For all the three years I was there, the college paid for me to have disposable needles and syringes. If I did not spend the money, they spent it for me. If I did not tell them when I was ready for the next cheque, they sent me one regardless. The senior tutor even went to the lengths of proposing a push-button hypo alarm system connected with Addenbrooke's for the Trinity house in which I lived. When I said it would be no good because I would be too paralysed to reach it, he suggested the creation of a Heath Robinson-type automatic honey-drip from the ceiling and thereafter his imagination moved into the realms of the surreal. I was grateful for all the ideas, however fantastic and impractical, and I especially appreciated being so protected by an institution – a new experience for me.

By now my understanding of hypoglycaemia had developed dramatically. As well as ghastliness, madness, paralysis, coma, suspended existence and the fearful awareness of all that, I had also just experienced the worst facet of a mental hypo: the transformation of time into hell.

Of all the characteristics of hypoglycaemia, this is the most impossible to describe and I feel thankful that so few people can know what it is like. I found out one morning when I went home for the weekend and was doing some gardening. It was sunny and I was digging the vegetable patch, wearing shorts and a shirt. I felt tired, hot and depressed. And the more I dug, the more depressed I felt. Everyone's hypos are different and I now know that misery, for me, is one of the first signs of a hypo. But I did not know that then and went on digging, telling myself angrily to snap out of it. I pulled at the weeds, but could not get them to budge. I hated the weeds for being so stubborn, I hated the soil, I looked at how much of the patch I still had to dig and hated being alive.

I went into the house and took a shandy out of the fridge. If I had got an ordinary one, with sugar in it, I would have been all right. But my brain was not working properly and I got a can of diabetic shandy, without sugar, and drank that lying on the lawn, distraught with misery. I lay there and went into that terrible place and the waves closed over my head. I was there for hours. I went further and further away from my life and the time I spent there got longer, and turned into days. I knew it was hell because there was no way out; I would never escape. I was there for years. I went through years of life, years when no one could touch or help me. The terror of that time turned into evil – with no hope, no happiness and nothing good – comes back to me as I write.

My mother says I lay on the lawn for less than five minutes. She tried to bring me round and when she could not, called the doctor. I then astounded her by getting up before he arrived and going into the kitchen as if nothing was wrong and eating a peach. I cannot imagine how I managed it. When the doctor came I was sitting in the kitchen eating a

144

biscuit, trying not to take in what had happened. As soon as I was back in human time, the other, evil time faded to a shadow, thank God. But I could not stop thinking about it for days afterwards and could not stop a terror of it happening again from taking root and adding another dimension to the beast.

I crossed a threshold that day and can never go back again. I used to be fascinated by time and the only bit of St Augustine I ever liked was the last chapter of his *Confessions* with its hypnotic section on time, memory and infinity. But now I can only read it with my head; my heart runs away. I believe in God but the thought of eternity fills me with horror: I dread the thought of anything, even heaven, going on without end.

9

By Force I Live

By force I live, in will I wish to die.
(Robert Southwell, *Life is but Losse*)

In the twelve years I have been diabetic I have been to places that do not exist and experienced impossible dimensions of time. I have alternately become someone else, gone mad and ceased to exist. I am rather proud of my hypos. Indeed, I would hate to think of anyone having hypos like them. Yet despite all that, they have had their good harvest too, in showing me a side to people which I would otherwise have missed.

It is odd, how my having diabetes has changed my attitude to people. When it was diagnosed, I expected that people's attitude to me would change, but not that I myself would become so much more sympathetic. I have much more time now for complaints like tiredness, depression and weakness. When I came back from India I thought they were the complaints of affluence, indulgence and self-pity; I had little patience with them. But I would hesitate to make that judgement now: you never know what lies behind them or to what depths they have taken people.

I love it when someone says I look well. I used to think it was a bit *sportif* but now I am pleased. When you feel invisibly ill, the great thing is to keep it invisible. Michael was right about being above it all, and more so than ever when you are in fact down below it. When people ask, 'How are you?' I always say I am fine, whatever I feel like, except with close friends who really want to know. By 'above it all' standards, being alive is the only fact of any importance and if I am alive, the answer is that I am fine.

There is nothing like a close run with death to bring that home. I had one just before I left Cambridge. One morning I was carted off to hospital in a bad hypo, paralysed from top to toe. All I could move were my eyes, which had multiple vision, and my head, which rolled helplessly from side to side like an apple on a string. I was semi-conscious but remember the drive to hospital with one of those ever-adorable ambulancemen covering me with an extra blanket, as I was freezing cold, and describing me over his intercom to the hospital as 'diabetic, female, unable to move and aged about twenty-one'. I was delighted with this last comment and tried to smile at him, but I could only make my lips twitch pathetically. When we arrived at the hospital, they told the doctor I was diabetic and he looked into my eyes and said, 'She's going into a coma. We'd better give her some insulin quickly.' I was terror-struck and tried to tell him I needed sugar, not insulin; if he gave me the injection it would finish me off. I made a noise and tried to shake my head, which tumbled about hopelessly. The doctor came up with a syringe full of insulin. He rubbed my arm with a sterile swab ready for the injection and I changed my prayer from 'Please God, help me' to 'Please God, stop him.' I was frantic. My head shook crazily and I tried with everything in me to say *no*. There was a nurse there who kept wiping the sweat off my forehead with a damp cloth and telling me not to worry.

I gave a maximum capacity moan as he rubbed the vein he was going to inject and the nurse said, 'Doctor, I think she's trying to say no. I wonder if there's something wrong.'

147

I gave an affirmative moan and blessed her in my heart. The doctor looked at me doubtfully and said, 'I don't think so but perhaps we'd better do a blood test just to be sure.'

My heart eased off to a thousand beats a second. I am an inveterate devotee of life and knew I had been reprieved for a bit more of it. The doctor pricked my finger, expressed surprise but no particular interest that it showed a low blood sugar, not a high one, and said, 'We'll give you some glucose instead.'

He shoved a syringe full of glucose into my arm and within seconds I could wiggle everything I had. I thanked the nurse and then the doctor. The nurse looked embarrassed; while the doctor just said, 'That's all right.' He was a cool customer and had a moustache. A lot of doctors do nowadays, just like policemen.

I suddenly thought of a line from an Anouilh play we had learnt at school, *Il faut jouer la vie pour se sentir vivre*, although I didn't really share the sentiment. *Je me sens vivre n'importe quoi*, but I must say I saw what Anouilh meant extra specially at that moment.

Mistakes are easy to make in diabetes. In my time I have injected myself with wine, water, surgical spirit and even cold cream – when I was so hypo that I did not know what I was doing. I have broken injected needles off at the hilt, so that I had to pluck out the end with tweezers. I have injected myself before a meal and had the meal delayed for an hour by a bomb scare. I have had my syringe sat on by a large man taking me to dinner with his friends, which turned out to be inordinately starchy, starting with spaghetti and ending with cake: all that carbohydrate and no insulin! The friends were East European and I ate it all, frightened that a refusal would be hurtful. I had an injection when I got home and all was well.

While holidaying in Scotland I ran out of proper needles

and had to borrow a horse needle from the crofter next door. It was gigantic and I banged the plunger of the syringe with a shoe to get it through my skin and had to bandage the hole it left afterwards. I have eaten a packet of sandwiches, paper wrapping, cardboard and all, on a station platform in a hypo frenzy. I have walked out of a shop with the biscuits I needed, without paying for them. I have got on to a bus and lain down on the floor, smiling up at the people stepping over me to get out. I have thrown my shopping all over the road, read *The Times* three times without understanding a word of it, put supper in the oven and never taken it out, gone to sleep in the back of a car and woken up hypo, telling the psychiatrist and his wife who were driving me that they were mad. I never thought the day would come when I would want life to be boring.

Although a part of my brain often knows that I am feeling hypo, the state itself stops me being able to do anything about it. Nor am I able to admit my problem to anyone I am with. If asked, I always deny that anything is wrong. It is this inability to explain to others that I need sugar once a hypo has started which baffles everyone around me. Even when they can see I am not myself, my constant denials leave them powerless to act. I seem odd but am nevertheless coherent to outsiders, so they leave me alone when I ask to be left.

Just recently I played tennis with someone who knew I was diabetic but who did not really understand what it involved. After a hopeless game, when I was feeling hypo, saw double and hit nothing, he blithely left me to cycle off by myself. I had travelled about two hundred yards, wobbling and wilting, with cars honking at me as I drifted all over the road, when a small internal voice told me that I was going to fall off. True to form, my hypo self went ahead and did so. I did it quite gracefully, all things considered, in slow motion,

149

resplendent in my tennis whites. My racket, my bike and I lay in a crumpled heap on the road. A car screeched to a halt just behind me and I noticed that its tyres were smoking. The driver jumped out and yelled, 'Are you bloody mad or what?'

I do not blame him, and distantly observed several more vehicles performing similar emergency stops behind his car. I told myself that I was hypo and that my hair was getting dirty, lying on the road. Then a motor-bike screeched up, driven by a young punk with hard flesh icons on his jacket. He jumped off, helped me up and walked me to the pavement, going back to rescue my paraphernalia and to tell the furious driver to rearrange his face. He then asked me what was wrong, while all the cars roared away. I said I was diabetic. To my surprise, the punk was tickled.

'I know all about that,' he said. 'Me girlfriend, 'er mate was diabetic. What you need is sugar. Got any in 'ere?'

He opened my handbag and rummaged through it until he found a tube of Dextrose tablets which he waved triumphantly to the little crowd now gathered, uneasy and interested, around us. We sat down on the pavement and the lovely punk fed me Dextrose until I felt well enough to say, 'your feet are enormous' – which they were.

'Not bad, is they?' he said proudly and showed me his boots, laced to half-way up his shins. When I was together again, he watched me cycle away before getting on his motor-bike and screeching off, waving a gloved hand as he went.

Unembarrassable people like him are a tonic to diabetics, who struggle with an awkward and anti-social condition. I try and do injections inconspicuously but sometimes it attracts too much attention to go out to the ladies just before a meal and so I do them under the table – through my tights. Fishnet are the easiest because you can go through the holes, but any sort will do. Trousers or a long skirt are harder; you

150

have to pull the waist down and inject into your stomach. At a formal dinner in Cambridge once, when I found myself in a long dress which I could not pull up without a lot of problems, and with long sleeves too narrow to push up, I did the injection into my hand. Never again. There is not enough flesh and the insulin stayed under my skin in a blushing cushion, red and sore for a week.

You can never tell how people are going to react. I am so used to the whole business that I sometimes forget what a shock it must be for people to see me injecting myself. During a night at the theatre, I once did an injection in the ladies cloakroom and explained as I did so to someone who was looking at me oddly that it was insulin. She promptly went into the lavatory and threw up.

Other people could not care less. I go to a Benedictine monastery for Easter each year and the first year I went, no one knew me or anything about my condition. At prayers one morning, I stood next to a tall, elderly monk who guided me kindly through the impenetrable maze of his prayer book. His bespectacled face was at such a height above mine that I thought he would not see if I did an injection there and then, which I had to do as breakfast was straight after prayers; it was either there or in the refectory. I bent my head piously and went ahead.

'I hope that doesn't hurt,' he said.

I looked up and there was the bespectacled face, bent piously over me, watching with great interest.

'No,' I whispered, flushing.

'Good,' he whispered. And he winked before he went. He had not even asked me what it was I was injecting.

I always think doctors must find diabetes a bore, but strangely enough those who specialise in it use the adjective 'interesting' more than any other. They evidently find an intellectual appeal in working out a condition which involves delicate mathematical balance, the detection and prediction of patterns and the manipulation of forces to produce an equilibrium. The diabetic doctors I have met seem cleverer and more enquiring than the average.

Three summers ago, when I got back from Scotland, I went to a clinic at the John Radcliffe Hospital in Oxford, expecting to see one of the fistful of registrars who usually looked after me. But a tall, handsome doctor, who had only appeared once or twice during my previous sessions at the clinic, came up and introduced himself, saying that he was going to look after me. Edward is an expert on hypoglycaemia – dividing his time between medical research and a few select hypo patients – and is the most concerned doctor I have ever come across. He understands more about hypoglycaemia than any non-diabetic I have ever met, and once told me that his aim in life is to eliminate it from the face of the earth. He gives himself hypos in the cause of research, which leaves me speechless with admiration. I am privileged to have been under his care at the Radcliffe and desolate now that he has left to be a consultant in London.

I do not know when I will be in there again, for I seem to have passed the peak of my hypo career. There will undoubtedly be other peaks yet to come, but this one will do, for it added a new dimension to my hypoglycaemic experience. As a combination of the physical and the even more accursed mental hypo, it was devastating. I was meeting a friend for lunch at a local pub and cycled there feeling vague. We bought drinks and took them into the garden to wait for our food. I kept asking Gill to repeat herself because I could not hear what she was saying. Then I put my head down on the table and started convulsing, spilling the drinks and kicking the wall. Gill ran off and phoned the doctor who told her to bring me up to the hospital. She told me to get up and was surprised when I did, normally, and followed her. She hailed a taxi in the street and we got in. That taxi ride up to the John

Radcliffe is burnt into my memory. I writhed and jerked and stretched, my head on the floor one minute and pressed up under the ceiling the next. The driver turned round and said, 'Jesus Christ. Lock the doors.'

For little patches I lay still, then convulsed again, howling. Gill sat frightened and quiet until we reached the hospital, where I keeled over and came to with a glucose drip in my vein. They kept me in hospital overnight, which they had never done before after a hypo, and told me that 'fitting' is a bad sign. I have had 'fitting' hypos occasionally since then, and do not need any convincing: one even left me without the usual feeling of serenity after the attack, the beast's only redeeming feature.

It was in Amsterdam, where I had taken my mother for a weekend. We had walked ourselves off our feet and, in my case, out of sugar. My mother says she knew I was 'going off' but as it was nearly dinner-time she thought the best thing was to get to a restaurant quickly and give me something to eat. The trouble was, I kept refusing all the restaurants we went past, saying I did not want food. Finally she just dragged me into one, where I started to go into truly epic convulsions. I do not recall anything more until I came round to find a burly Dutchman pinning my arms behind my back in a wrestling hold and my mother pouring a sweet drink down my throat. She was sweating and her hands were shaking. Poor thing; I had not told her about this latest development and she was very upset.

However, I recovered quickly and we ordered hamburgers. The kind Dutchman and his wife nodded and smiled at us from their table nearby, the wife clucking sympathetically. I felt much better but instead of feeling flooded with life as I usually do after a hypo I felt sick of everything; unspeakably sick of living like this, sick of being alone with it, and finally, sick at the thought of it going on. I made myself cheer up, mainly for my poor mother's sake, while the Dutch couple finished their meal and left. On their way out the man came over to me and said, 'God bless you in your life.'

To stop myself bursting into floods of tears I just said, 'Thank you.'

I have been fortunate about hypos at work. With such brittle diabetes I doubt if I would have managed a serious career without a great many problems. Mercifully, I have never wanted a serious career and have been lucky with the jobs I have done. In Cambridge I was working by myself, which was ideal from a diabetic point of view though humanly speaking too solitary. But by the time I left I had written my first book and had started doing freelance writing, journalism and broadcasting. Of those three only broadcasting is directly vulnerable to diabetic damage; writing I can do in my own time – and on my own – but broadcasting involves other people and can be problematic.

My diabetes has so far caused just one minor hiccup in my broadcasting, however – when I had a mild hypo during a recording session for the *Today* programme. In the studio I found that I could not read the script without slurring and dragging my words. But as the programme was not going out live, no damage was done, and my kind producer arranged for the session to be taken later: she put me in a taxi and asked me to record the talk at Radio Oxford so that someone there could forward the tape to London. Her attitude was heart-warming and I was most grateful, for I wanted to make programmes as long as I could, and with that kind of support diabetes can stop being an insurmountable hindrance.

But I soon found that living by freelance broadcasting alone was impossible, and I needed a steadier source of income. So I got a job teaching, two-thirds time, which gave me enough money to pay the rent and enough time to write and make programmes. My post was at a high-powered girls' school with an excellent teaching standard. I was lucky to get it.

I was fine for two years. As far as the school was concerned, my diabetes was more or less under control. Then all at once, towards the end of the 1983 Easter term, it went down the plug. I do not know why. It is always brittle but suddenly it decided to break up completely. My sugar level plummeted during lessons and I would hear myself getting slow and disconnected, announcing facts at random, tapering off arguments into nothing, being silly. The girls were impeccable. They put up their hands politely, got permission to go out, and came back with one of the staff, who gave me sweet tea in the staff-room. But next term was 'A' and 'O' level term, and neither staff nor pupils could afford to lose work time. I had not missed any more school than anyone else in the two and a half years I had been there, but I had the permanent potential for missing a great deal. And to cap it all, I had ended that particularly disastrous week by sitting in the staff-room and not being able to get up. Someone helped me into the cloakroom, where I twisted about, clutching on to coats, until an ambulance came. A thoughtful member of staff made the ambulancemen wait until the girls were all in lessons before I was ignominiously humped off through the school gates on a stretcher.

I was unconscious by then and did not know anything about my colleague's kindness. I came round in hospital with a glucose drip in my arm and somehow sensed that I had finally overstepped the mark and would be sacked. The idea that contact with illness can be a valuable part of education is a luxury in a prestigious academic school. I happen to think it is a good idea and I am glad that my own school included all sorts, from the talented to the simple-minded and the crippled. But the pressures on performance in an academic school are much heavier and I do not blame the headmistress for

155

thinking I was too much of a liability. I was, and still am a risk.

That afternoon, after being pumped full of glucose, I slipped back into a coma and came to an hour later with another glucose drip in my arm. Unfortunately for the headmistress, however, I did not maintain that standard of decrepitude and the next day I went back to my duties at the school and displayed my well-being to everyone by charging up and down in the mud during the staff-pupil hockey match. Despite this, the headmistress called me into her office minutes after the game had ended and regretfully asked me to leave.

I had been wishing for some time that I could again try to survive on freelance work alone and now the decision had been taken for me: I was to depart immediately with a term's pay in lieu of notice.

I did not mind my dismissal but a great many people did, which created a strained atmosphere in the staff-room, especially as the girls now had to make do with a stand-in teacher a term before their exams. As far as I was concerned though, a term with full pay and no work was perfect. I wished I could make it a permanent arrangement. I could have made out a strong case for fighting dismissal in those circumstances, as some of the staff and girls wanted me to do, but my heart wasn't in it.

There was a diabetic teacher at a nearby school, and an epileptic one, and their ups and downs were accepted as temporary and unavoidable. Some people regarded my dismissal angrily as a step towards a Nazi type of society where only perfect human specimens are desirable. It was kind of them but it embarrassed me nevertheless. I would undoubtedly have supported them if it had been someone else in my shoes but as it was I felt awkward and shamefaced about the whole affair.

I felt sorry for the headmistress and sympathised with the dilemma in which she had found herself. But above all I hated leaving the girls. They wrote petitions to the school governors and the day I left they festooned me with cards, plants and flowers. They still drop in sometimes, two years later, to tell me the school news and show me their new leg-warmers. I still miss them badly.

10

The Roads are Pretty Choppy

When you're riding in my Uncle Joe's jalopy,
Better hang on tight 'cos the roads are pretty choppy.
(Kit Wright, *Uncle Joe's Jalopy*)

Diabetes must be almost as old as humanity itself but it has only been an English institution for fifty years. It is now an official subculture. Besides the natural camaraderie of its doctors and patients, there is a British Diabetic Association, complete with newspaper, clubs, dieticians, medical and legal advice, video cassettes, and even diabetic tea-towels. I ought to belong to the BDA, which is obviously a marvellous organisation, but I do not.

I ought also to think of myself as a diabetic but I do not. Instead, I think of myself as someone who happens to have diabetes and I would rather not belong to an association in which diabetes is the *sine qua non*; there are better ways to be counted. But the BDA is an admirable body. It has over 100,000 members – a sixth of the diabetic population of Britain – who would obviously not belong unless it helped them. What is more, it was founded by the writer H. G. Wells and is therefore interesting as well as important.

Wells was a diabetic and in 1933 his doctor persuaded him to write to *The Times* asking diabetics to organise an association for fellow sufferers and provide it with funds. The response was overwhelming and in January 1934 twenty-four doctors and diabetics met in Wells' London flat to form the British Diabetic Association, which was the first self-help organisation in Britain and the model for many more. Every self-respecting condition – multiple sclerosis, deafness and blindness, to name but a few – has an equivalent solidarity association nowadays.

Over sixty diabetic associations have been formed all over the world, and their aim is twofold: to give diabetics all the information they need to cope with their condition and to lobby governments to improve diabetic care. In the 1930s there were no special provisions for diabetics in Britain other than a few overcrowded hospital clinics, and by 1938 there were still only twenty-eight registered diabetic clinics in this country. Many areas did not have one at all and sufferers relied on their local doctors, who often had little experience of diabetic care. The BDA, with Wells as its president, fought for free medical care and in 1948, when the National Health Service was set up, urged that the number of diabetic clinics be increased. It has kept up the pressure ever since and today England can boast over a thousand.

The latest target for BDA pressure on the National Health is blood test sticks. At present they are not available on prescription and one has to rely on a tame hospital doctor to provide supplies from hospital stocks. The BDA has been campaigning for years to get them put on the prescribed medication list but so far the government has refused, on the grounds that they are too expensive. They are indeed pro-hibitively so, but I would have thought it cheaper in the long run to supply them free, because they help people keep closer control over their diabetes and so avoid comas and the resultant emergency dash to hospital – which is far more costly.

I remain eternally grateful to the National Health Service for everything it provides – insulin, syringes and constant medical care. I could not ask for more. I do not even pay prescription charges because I am an habitual offender and therefore exempt, even if my prescription has nothing to do with diabetes. I am an unqualified supporter of the National Health. How could I be anything else? And by default I suppose I must also be a supporter of the BDA because a lot of National Health facilities are the direct result of BDA campaigning, especially of campaigns undertaken in the early days under Wells' leadership.

Wells was a great asset to the BDA. He was at the height of his popularity as a writer in the mid 1930s and gave diabetes invaluable media status. He made mincemeat of the traditional defeatist attitude that diabetics were doomed to die of their condition, incapable and unemployable. Ever since Wells' pioneering efforts the BDA has always had a public figure as its president (the present one being Sir Harry Secombe) and in 1952 the Queen became its patron.

There is a BDA quarterly newspaper aptly called *Balance* which has articles and pictures on everything to do with diabetes. I cannot bear it. When I was first diagnosed as a diabetic, I was told by various doctors that I should join the BDA but when I saw a copy of *Balance* I knew I could not. The front page of the issue I saw had a picture of a diabetic girl of about my age, standing on a beach somewhere warm and sunny, with an article on how well she had managed to handle unfamiliar carbohydrates on her holiday, counting a chunk of pineapple as the equivalent of an apple. The air of 'you too can be a normal human being' was suffocating. It would never have occurred to me to think twice before going abroad and eating whatever turned up or took my fancy. I simply could not read the quarterly after that, though I am sure that it helps other people. I have seen some recent copies and they have good advice, interesting recipes, a problem page and morale-boosting articles. It is just that I do not want reassurance of my own normality which is, in the main, what *Balance* tries cheerfully and determinedly to provide.

That is also why I do not belong to one of the BDA's 250 local units in Britain. These units organise voluntary get-togethers, provide talks on living with diabetes, visits to elderly diabetics and, most important of all, funds for research. On the question of funds, however, I count myself as a whole-hearted BDA supporter. It does not get any money from the government, relying entirely on subscriptions and donations.

In the end, research must be the most important aspect of diabetic medicine. It was Banting and Best's research into the causes of diabetes that led to the discovery of insulin and thus to the saving of over fifty million lives. Research into causes and treatments, if not cures, is more vital than ever now that public money is harder to come by. So the BDA invests in advertising. There are diabetic Christmas cards and information posters to raise funds; there are meetings, films and exhibitions, all geared to increase public consciousness of diabetes and offer practical help to the sufferers.

But despite a concerted public information campaign, most people's understanding of the condition remains limited – usually to an awareness that diabetics have to be careful about what they eat. There are a lot of diabetic cookery books (with dreadful titles like *Measure for Measure* and *Carbohydrate Countdown*). I do not use them myself, but I must admit that some of the diabetic recipes I have seen are excellent.* They give the number of carbohydrates and calories in each dish, use a variety of alternative sweeteners to sugar and go out of their way to give recipes for all the things one would normally think of as forbidden: sponge puddings, mousses, scones and cakes.

Quite a few diabetic recipes have much in common with the high fibre recipes in vogue at the moment. They use

*During the war diabetic recipes were a godsend. The BDA newspaper was then called the *Diabetic Journal* and its recipes and tips helped diabetics struggling with rationing. The BDA also got the government to introduce special rations for diabetics.

161

grated carrot and apple instead of sugar, All Bran instead of brown sugar, wholemeal instead of white flour. The recipes are much more inventive than they used to be: when I got diabetes I was given a booklet about diet which contained some recipes and they were a depressing experience. I started to make a lemon meringue pie to cheer myself up. But by the time I had squashed up unsweetened biscuits to make the base, whipped up egg whites and saccharin to make the top and begun making an unspeakable lemon filling with slimming lemonade, the only way to cheer up was to throw the hateful concoction away.

Travel with diabetes need not be a problem but it has plenty of problematic potential. The BDA has now extended the scope of its efforts to include advice on travel, holidays and emigration. There are pamphlets on how to cope with jet lag and time differences and what to do if you drop your insulin in Italy, Ireland, Norway – or indeed anywhere else in Europe. If you travel on a train where the buffet has run out of sandwiches or closed down you can easily go hypo. Air travel is easier because airlines spend most of their time feeding passengers anyway and all you have to do is leave what you do not need. Though God knows what would happen in a hijack. More mundanely, the crucial thing when travelling by air is to keep your syringe, insulin, needles and some carbohydrate in your hand baggage because if you pack the equipment away in a suitcase you will not see it again until some time after you land.

I carry Dextrose and sweets around with me in my handbag, which I clutch fanatically, like a terrorist clutching her bomb. When going through customs the best thing to do is tell the customs officer you are diabetic before he seizes your syringe and needles and locks you up for being a drug addict.

Most European countries will treat diabetic emergencies in hospital free of charge, but not all. Greece, for instance, charges for doctor and hospital treatment, insulin, oral

162

hypoglycaemic tablets, and the use of an ambulance. They will sometimes waive the charges but it is not a good idea to push your luck. I went to Greece in the spring of 1983 and took a spare bottle of insulin with me which I put in the hotel fridge. It was just as well I did. I carried the rest of my insulin around with me and it turned rancid in the heat; the usually clear liquid went murky and I found white flakes floating around in it. I threw the rancid bottles away and resorted to the fridge bottle, wrapping it in a wet flannel and taking it with me whenever I went out for the day. I finished the holiday with only about two shots of insulin to spare.

Most of Europe uses pork insulin, unlike Britain where beef insulin is the norm. Pork insulin is stronger than the beef variety and consequently if you change to it you need to use less. The BDA publicises precise details of how to make the changeover together with a pamphlet with translations into nine languages of the following life-saving announcement: 'I am a diabetic and am taking insulin. If I am found ill or fainting please give me two tablespoonfuls of sugar in water. If I do not recover, please call a doctor or an ambulance immediately.'

Doctors dish out these cards to diabetics and I always carry one around in my handbag. It has often proved useful. In the summer of 1983 I went to a friend's wedding and cycled from the church up a long hill to the house where the reception was being held. Half-way up, I could not go on. I put my bike down on the road and lay down beside it. It just happened that a police car was behind me and it stopped to disgorge two young policemen. They asked me if there was anything wrong and I did not answer. One of them said, 'Have you got a medical condition?' I nodded but could not reply when he asked me what it was.

I take back everything I ever said about the police. This one opened my handbag, apologising as he did so, and rummaged through the contents until he found my diabetic card,

163

whereupon he disappeared into a nearby shop and re-emerged a minute later with a cup of sweet milk, while his colleague kept me company. I drank it and immediately felt better. But the police had the bit between their teeth and would not let me cycle on until I had been taken to the hospital in their car, and been given still more sugar and an all-clear from a doctor. Then they drove me back to my bike and I thanked them, wishing that they could know how much they had helped me.

The diabetic card also has other, more pedestrian uses. For example, you have to show it whenever you buy syringes in a chemist. My local chemist knows me and does not usually bother to ask me for mine, but big chemists make a point of it – though they never used to. For the first few years I bought needles and syringes *ad lib*. On the rare occasions when someone asked me to prove I was diabetic I would show them the insulin in my handbag, or a syringe, which is not ideal evidence, for it can only prove that you are a drug addict, not necessarily an insulin one. But it is a starting point *in extremis* and you can usually talk people into believing you. I showed a busy London chemist my British Library Reading Room card by mistake the other day and he produced the syringes I wanted at once!

The alternative means of advertising your diabetes is a Medic Alert disc. It has the international medical symbol on one side – a snake twined round a pole – and, on the other, the word diabetes and a phone number which automatically puts callers through to information about your condition. It is for use in case of accidents, but what if you crash miles away from a phone? Besides, it is dear: £13.80 for the disc on a bracelet or necklace and £35.00 if you want it in silver.

Proclaiming your condition is a bore. But you have to. If you do not declare your diabetes to insurance companies it can invalidate your policies. It is only since 1928 that diabetics have been able to get life insurance policies at all. I would never insure my life but seven years ago I bought a motor-bike and wanted to insure that. I filled in an insurance form which asked you to put a tick if you suffered from any of the ailments listed at the bottom of the page. The list included epilepsy and heart disease but not diabetes. Like a fool I told the broker that I had diabetes and he rang up all the insurance companies he could think of to ask them if they would insure me. All of them refused except one, which would only insure me at six times the normal premium. The next year I renewed the policy without mentioning my diabetes, and paid the normal rate though, if found out, my insurance would have been invalidated.

It would be stupid and unfair not to declare diabetes when applying for a job. If you declare it, then your employer is expected to 'absorb predictable absences', as the law puts it; that is to say, be tolerant when you need time off. Application forms for jobs in the BBC ask you to tick which of a list of ailments you have, and the first on the list is diabetes. But that does not mean diabetics cannot work for the BBC; they know I have diabetes and have always been kind and tolerant. When I told my producer I was diabetic he asked me what it entailed and what he should do if I got ill. That is the ideal attitude. It takes all the mystique out of the problem and relaxes you because you know help will be there if you need it. You worry less and work better. Most employers are willing to hire diabetics unless they are very unstable, and most large companies are prepared to include diabetics in their pension schemes because any risks are diluted in the large number of employees; smaller companies and banks are less willing.

I have every sympathy with employers. I know from personal experience how much trouble diabetes can cause at work, so I do not blame those who regard it as too much of a liability. But I also know that even with brittle diabetes the trouble is quickly and easily put right; in most jobs it need be nothing more than a short-lived, albeit recurring, nuisance.

I can only think of a few jobs that would really be impossible for a diabetic to do. Motor racing, I should think. And probably driving buses, trains and aeroplanes too; even momentary hypoglycaemia while driving could kill everyone on board. I remember reading a newspaper report some years ago about a man who was a stable diabetic and had been driving for years without any trouble. For some reason he had been switched from beef to pork insulin, which meant he needed less of it. I do not know what went wrong; maybe he forgot to take less insulin to compensate for the difference in strength. But at any rate he went hypo and drove his car over the edge of Hammersmith flyover and was killed. Poor, poor man.

Diabetes debars entrance to the armed forces, the police, the merchant navy and the protection services, such as fire brigade and ambulance. That all seems fair enough. I am not sure I would want to have an insulin-dependent diabetic operating on me but, surgery apart, I cannot see any argument against a diabetic doctor. I was looked after by a diabetic doctor for a while and found it unexpectedly enjoyable talking to her because her inside understanding was a comfort. Someone I know had a diabetic dentist and gave me a terrible account of sitting helpless in the chair while the dentist went hypo and waved the drill around, then collapsed on the floor, mercifully before he got in contact with the tooth.

Diabetics can and do play all sorts of sport. Apart from the fact that exercise can be enjoyable, it is also good for you and especially so if you are diabetic and need to use up sugar. In general, I dislike things that are good for me. I like things that are bad for me and nice. But sport is an exception because as far as I am concerned the point of it is enjoyment; any good it does is incidental and an added bonus. I am overcome with admiration for diabetics who excel in any sport. Hamilton Richardson, the tennis star who caused a sensation by beating the defending champion Budge Patty and winning Wimbledon in 1951, was a diabetic. So is Danny

McGrain, the Celtic and Scotland footballer. He has been diabetic since 1974, played in the World Cup that year in West Germany and captained Scotland in the 1982 World Cup in Spain. He has played for Scotland sixty-two times and says he feels so much better since taking insulin that he wishes he could have got diabetes years earlier. Bit much, that. I wish I knew a diabetic cricketer I could hero-worship.

Politics is a more difficult proposition. I suppose going hypo so often has made me pessimistic but I still don't think that an insulin-dependent diabetic should make important political decisions. God forbid that anyone liable to run short of blood sugar should have any responsibility for any of the armed forces.

However, there have been quite a few diabetic statesmen in recent political history. Nasser, for example, the late Egyptian President who ruled during the Suez Crisis of 1956, was diabetic, and Menachem Begin, Israel's Prime Minister from 1977 to 1983, has diabetes as well as a serious heart condition. I was also horrified to discover that Khrushchev was yet another diabetic. I do not know whether he took insulin; if he did, we are lucky to be here. A hypoglycaemic with his finger on the button does not bear contemplation.

Andropov was diabetic too, but the Russians are so pathologically secretive about their politicians that no one knows for sure whether he was insulin-dependent or not. In the last year of his life he had all the symptoms of long-term diabetes: exhaustion, weight loss, blood pressure and heart trouble and, most serious of all and most widely publicised, kidney failure. If he also suffered from hypoglycaemia on top of all that, I am sorry for him. He died a horrible death. Even the Politburo cannot cure diabetes and I am sorry to think of him having had to live with both of them.

About six or seven years ago it suddenly seemed to be fashionable to allege that famous people from history were

167

epileptic: Julius Caesar because he had 'the falling sickness'; the prophet Jeremiah because he was cataleptically gloomy; Francis Bacon because he had visionary moments before allegedly writing Shakespeare's plays. I enjoyed the lunacy of it all. Now I understand its fascination too, and have cultivated a new, diabetic perspective on history.

I was recently researching into the Catholic Church in the 19th century and found that Cardinal Wiseman, the first Catholic hierarch in England since the Reformation, was a diabetic. It changed the way I thought about him. He was a huge, florid, confident Catholic, of quite a different complexion from the old English Catholics who had survived three centuries of persecution by cultivating religious reticence and reserve. Wiseman worked on what he called the 'couleur de rose' principle; he was an optimist and he was flamboyant. He went to the consecration of Southwark Catholic Cathedral in 1848 dressed in full episcopal purple, in a coach drawn by four white horses, waving to the crowds like a monarch.

But by 1860 he was a different man. Insulin had yet to be discovered and diabetes had begun to erode him. He lost his *joie de vivre* and became moderate, acceptable, sluggish. He had one heart attack after another and when, in 1865, it became clear that he was dying, the public looked back on his former excesses as a departed glory. They forgave him everything in the shadow of his diabetes. Even Gladstone, who was dour, righteous Protestantism personified, went to see him on his deathbed. Characteristically Wiseman continued to work right up until the end although he could not concentrate for more than five minutes at a time and regularly fell asleep during conversations. He lay on his bed like a beached whale, festooned with rosaries and crucifixes. When he died his old enemies wept. I used to be savagely critical of Wiseman but now I can only be sympathetically and affectionately critical – both as an historian and a diabetic.

Across the centuries, the number of famous people who

may have been diabetic is, in all probability, very high. Up until the late 19th century it was common to attribute people's deaths to 'wasting diseases' – a nebulous and all-encompassing term – which could include diabetes. But when you come across someone who definitely *was* diabetic, it is fascinating. As far as I am concerned, it is the only interesting point about the Liberal MP Richard Haldane, who helped found Bristol and Liverpool universities and made the Imperial College of Science and Technology part of London University. He was one of the first diabetics to take insulin, which gave him a few extra years of life until he died in 1929.

Diabetes adds the final touch of pathos to Stan Laurel, the thin half of Laurel and Hardy, and to Richard Hearne, whom I used to love as Mr Pastry for his sad face and self-sacrificial humour. Lionel Bart, who wrote the musical *Oliver*, is a diabetic and so is the Shakespearian actor Alan Howard, who keeps sugar lumps hidden behind the scenery in case he suddenly needs topping up.

The most intriguing possibility in the spot-the-famous-diabetic game is Elvis Presley. The BDA have him listed as a diabetic but I cannot find any concrete evidence to support this, though circumstantial evidence abounds. Elvis died of a heart attack when he was only forty-two, having suffered from hypertension (high blood pressure) for years. That could be due to his frenzied life-style but it could also be because he was diabetic. Towards the end of his life he cancelled shows, talked his way through numbers he did not have the energy to sing, and twice collapsed on stage. He was so tired he could not stand for long and had to sit down. It sounds familiar.

But if Elvis was diabetic and full of sugar, as those symptoms suggest, he is unlikely to have taken insulin for it, which would have been one possible explanation for the frequent injections he gave himself in the last years of his life.

169

His bodyguards and other members of the Presley entourage have recounted how he was always shooting himself up in the arms and legs, leaving little plastic syringes everywhere. But if he was taking insulin, he would surely not have been too sugary all the time and in need of constant injections. Except that he did go off periodically on huge eating binges, locking himself in a room with mountains of hamburgers, ice-creams and junk food of every description. I suppose it would be just about possible to get the worst of diabetes both ways by doing that: injecting and being hypo one minute (he was apparently once admitted to hospital in the year he died, 1977, with hypoglycaemia) and over-eating until you are hyperglycaemic the next – which would also account for his expanding size.

But if Elvis was diabetic, why did he find it necessary to be so secretive about it? There had been rumours about his being a drug addict for years. He denied the rumours repeatedly but never said he was diabetic, which would have won him sympathy when he badly needed it. All things considered, I doubt if Elvis had diabetes. But if he did, he was the model of how not to cope with it.

For some reason, diabetes seems to be a characteristic of tough writers, Ernest Hemingway being the supreme example. He was in life much like the heroes of his novels – superhumanly rugged, battered but triumphant. Over the years he had countless serious illnesses and nearly as many accidents: two air-crashes left him with a broken spine, ruptured kidney and liver, and he also suffered a heart attack. But being Hemingway he walked away from it all. He was the life force incarnate, the masculine life force he idolised: a lover of brutal blood sports; passionate and defiant of death, which he called 'the old whore' and dreaded all his life.

By late 1956 Hemingway had developed very high blood pressure which aggravated his heart trouble and he was ordered to follow a strict diet. He used to proudly show visitors his swollen liver then burst out of his diet to drink exorbitantly. He was given electric shock treatment for depression, which had afflicted him for thirty years. He did not get diabetes until the last year of his life but it damaged him more than all his other complaints. He lost vast amounts of weight in no time. But even that was in keeping with his style; he had once lost seventeen pounds in one day fighting a giant sailfish. But losing sugar weight was something else. He became horribly depressed. He went from a big, burly embodiment of the outdoors to a frail wreck in a lunatic asylum, weeping because he could no longer write.

Hemingway's father had committed suicide. He too had developed diabetes and high blood pressure and one day had taken a gun and shot himself through the head. His suicide haunted Hemingway, whose own death had a ghastly inevitability about it. He went home from hospital and walked into the woods behind his house. In the old days he had walked miles through the hills, killing everything that moved. But on the morning of his death he hardly had the strength to carry his shotgun. He walked as far as he could then put the gun up to his head and pulled the trigger. Hemingway was the wrong design for diabetes.

In a way it is more interesting knowing about ordinary diabetics because it is easier to identify with them. Every so often diabetes gets into the media and when it does its public face is often traumatic. In legal cases, for example, diabetes always provides the stuff of controversy. However, you *can* plead diabetes in your defence if you are accused of a crime though to do so can be hazardous.

There was a much reported case just over twenty years ago involving a man accused of a serious crime pleading hypoglycaemia as his defence. This lawsuit – Watmore versus Jenkins – became the model for cases involving diabetics and its judgement set a precedent which, from a diabetic point of view, is disastrous. But it makes good reading. Watmore represented the police and for all I know may be the policeman who was nearly killed by Jenkins in the course of his nightmare drive which provoked the public prosecution. Jenkins was a diabetic who at the time of the drive in question, June 19th, 1961, had been taking insulin for eight years. He took a mixture of slow and very slow-acting insulin and was well stabilised. He was forty-six years old and had driven for twenty years without any trouble.

In February 1961 Jenkins went into Guy's Hospital, where he was a diabetic out-patient, with a bad attack of jaundice. By mid-May he had recovered and was back at work, taking more insulin than before because jaundice makes the liver produce more hydrocortisone (a chemical which works against insulin). Jenkins worked as a chartered accountant and on June 19th, after a normal day's work and normal meals, he left a client's house in Clapham at six forty-five to drive home to Coulsdon. The drive was described in thrillingly matter-of-fact language by the police.

Jenkins had no recollection of what happened after turning out of London Road into Carshalton Road, Mitcham Junction. What actually happened, according to the police statement, was that his car:

'proceeded in a southerly direction a distance of over five miles on roads of varying width and character . . . In London Road, Hackbridge, and London Road, Wallington, the car proceeded at 25 to 28 mph and veered from one side of the road to the other, and it hit the nearside kerb on one occasion. In Manor Road, Wallington, it went straight over the first set of traffic lights, narrowly missing a stationary car, and hit the nearside kerb again further along that road.' The car was next observed by a police constable [could this have been Constable Watmore?] in Woodcote

Grove Road, Coulsdon: 'The car was proceeding on the wrong side of the road, and it caused the police constable, who was going in the opposite direction on a motor cycle, to pull into the kerb and stop.' At this point the respondent [Jenkins] had already overshot his home turning by quarter of a mile.

A short time later, the driver of a northbound car who was traversing the railway bridge in Woodcote Grove Road had to take hasty evading action to avoid the respondent's car which swerved towards him on the wrong side of the road. It swerved back to its nearside and scraped that side of the railway bridge as it did so. The car then proceeded at approximately 40 mph diagonally across the road and struck a Ford car travelling in the opposite direction a glancing blow on its nearside. It finally crashed into the back of an Austin car parked by the offside kerb in front of the Co-operative Hall in Woodcote Grove Road near the junction of Chipstead Valley Road. The respondent's car was halted by the impact.

Now that is a driving offence worth committing. The police brought charges against Jenkins on three counts: driving a motor vehicle while unfit to drive through drink or drugs, driving a motor vehicle in a manner dangerous to the public and, finally, driving a motor vehicle without due care and attention. The case was heard by magistrates at Wallington who heard evidence from Jenkins' doctors at Guy's and the doctor at Purley Hospital. The latter had given him glucose when he was taken there 'in a confused and dangerous state and almost inarticulate' after his drive. The doctors agreed that Jenkins was hypo, but that this was not the result of the drug, insulin, which he had taken; it was the result of the altered function of his liver after jaundice, which caused an unpredictable insulin reaction. Jenkins had taken a normal dose of insulin and eaten normally;

173

therefore his hypo was not his fault. His plea was that he was not guilty because at the time of the offence he was in a state of automatism. The magistrates heard all the evidence, accepted his defence and found him not guilty on all three counts.

So far, so good, and very nice of the magistrates. Jenkins drove like a demon, felt like death and got away with it. No one was hurt. But the police appealed against the acquittal and the case was referred to the Divisional Court under the Lord Chief Justice, Lord Parker. All the evidence was presented again, but this time a different conclusion was reached. It was agreed that Jenkins should be acquitted of the first charge. The last charge was dropped, but the judges found Jenkins guilty of the second, namely dangerous driving.

They delivered judgement against him because they could not accept that he was 'in a state of automatism', a state which Justice J. Winn said was defined by law as 'involuntary movement of the body or limbs'. For some of his five-mile drive Jenkins must have been in control of his body or limbs and was therefore not in a state of automatism throughout. Justice Winn went on to remark drily, 'Questions of causation have always occupied and intrigued philosophers, but the law leaves them to be determined as matters of fact.' And in this case the fact was that Jenkins was driving his car dangerously, whether he meant to or not. The judges directed the magistrates to find Jenkins guilty of dangerous driving but in view of the special circumstances he was given an absolute discharge.

Thank God Jenkins was not penalised any further: his hypo – and subsequent events – had been punishment enough. But I think it was wrong that he was found guilty of dangerous driving. Clearly he was dangerous but I share the magistrates' original view that although he was actually driving the car, he was not *responsible* for what he did. Whether or not he was in a state of automatism is simply a matter of legal definition and if there is no legal definition to cover helpless hypoglycaemia I wish they would make one.

Had Jenkins gone hypo through his own fault, after deciding to risk skipping a meal or drinking without eating, say, then his innocence would have been open to doubt. That kind of culpable hypo is what happened to another diabetic brought before the courts in April 1973, and in this case I think the defendant was lucky to get away with it. Q was convicted of assault occasioning actual bodily harm. He was a diabetic who worked as a nurse at a psychiatric hospital, where he assaulted a patient, remembering nothing about it afterwards. His defence was that he was hypo and therefore – the recurring bugbear – in a state of automatism.

The judge ruled that the defence of automatism was not open to Q; his only defence was insanity. Understandably Q refused to plead insanity, changed his plea to guilty and then appealed against his conviction. The appeal court held that the judge's ruling was wrong. Common sense rebelled against a diabetic being declared insane; his mind might be temporarily aberrant but that is all. The court then went on to say that Q should have been allowed a defence of automatism because his temporary mental imbalance was caused by an external factor, namely insulin, and not by his diabetes.

That seems to me a false distinction. Diabetes and insulin are inseparable when a diabetic is taking insulin. And why should automatism be restricted to external causes? If his diabetes had caused his imbalance he could only have pleaded insanity, but because insulin had caused it, he had a let-out. Q was lucky. Especially since he had a history of hypoglycaemia, with twelve previously recorded hypos while he was working at the hospital, despite which he was stupid enough to miss a meal and have some drinks on the day of the assault. He was asking for hypoglycaemia – and fortunate that his case was handled by judges who evidently understood

175

nothing about the workings of diabetes. They confessed themselves incredulous that something as trivial as missing a meal could determine whether a man was responsible for his actions or not. I can believe it only too easily. The judges said they thought the rules and definitions in the case needed reconsidering. So do I.

The most horrific case I can think of involving insulin was one that was reported in the papers five or six years ago, though it had nothing to do with diabetes. A nurse was found guilty of killing patients in a geriatric hospital by injecting them with insulin. The case received a lot of coverage as some of the patients had apparently said to one nurse that they wanted to die. Consequently, the defendant pleaded not guilty because she claimed to have committed euthanasia, not murder. She had acted in accordance with the wishes of her patients.

My reaction was absolute. I regard euthanasia as murder, albeit of a comparatively understandable and kindly-motivated sort. But even if I held different views, I would still have considered the nurse injecting her patients with insulin a horrific crime. One newspaper gave a description of how insulin kills you, mentioning convulsions, sweating, mental confusion and 'distress'. I looked at the picture of an old lady sitting in a wheelchair looking sadly out of the window and thought of her in 'distress', hypo. The report said the nurse had given her patients 'repeated doses of insulin'. My blood ran cold. If the patients wanted to die before they were given their 'repeated doses', it was nothing to how much they must have wanted to die after them.

I imagined it was me sitting by the window going hypo, into an intensity of despair which I could never have imagined. The nurse was sent to prison. I felt sorry for her but appalled at what she had put her patients through. If she had ever experienced a shot of insulin herself, she would surely never have done what she did, even from the kindest of motives.

From the criminal point of view insulin is the perfect killer. It is the only untraceable drug. If you murder someone with arsenic or cyanide, it leaves traces in the blood, but insulin is invisible. It is not really a drug; it is a protein and therefore has no tangible presence; its only presence is in its effects. And for a nurse, it is easy to get hold of. Since 1980 it has also been available over the counter, without a prescription. It is easy to inject, lethal and, in substance, non-existent.

I read a crime novel once in which the murder was done by insulin. In one sense there ought to be more insulin murder novels; it is such a good means of killing. But it is too obscure a device for most readers and, at the same time, too pat and convenient. There is nothing more irritating than a crime novel where the solution is unbelievable. Before I was diabetic I would not have enjoyed an insulin-hinged crime novel. But now that I am, I wouldn't enjoy one for different reasons, though I must admit to a kind of gruesome fascination with reading anything to do with diabetes in newspapers, magazines and so on; especially when it involves controversy or violence.

Two years ago I felt my stomach tighten when I saw a story in a newspaper about the release from prison of a man who had been convicted of killing his wife with insulin. It was considered newsworthy because he was the second-longest serving prisoner in Britain but I thought it was newsworthy for its horror content alone. The man was released from Leyhill Open Prison near Bristol in early January 1984 after twenty-seven years in jail. Somehow I knew before I read it that he would turn out to be a former nurse. He had been jailed in 1957 for what the court had described as 'a perfect murder'; murder by insulin.

The man's wife drowned in her bath after falling into a coma. When the police arrived, they found her body in the bath, in a foetal sleeping position, which did not accord well with the husband's claim that he had found her under the water and had tried to give her artificial respiration. The pupils of her eyes were widely dilated, a well known symptom of acute hypoglycaemia. The police searched the house and found a pair of sweat-soaked ladies' pyjamas; sweating is another well known symptom of the condition. They also found two syringes, one of them still wet from recent use, and four hypodermic needles, wrapped in a handkerchief in a porcelain pot on a shelf above the door of the pantry.

The man confessed that he had given his wife an injection, and two post-mortems revealed four possible injection marks, two on each buttock. He claimed to have injected his wife with a drug to end her pregnancy; the post-mortems also revealed an eight-week foetus. If he was telling the truth, that is bad enough; if the prosecution was right and he murdered his wife and baby with insulin, it is unbearable.

The forensic scientists working on the case were unable to isolate any insulin crystals in the woman's body but found that over a thousand mice injected with extracts from the woman's body all suffered convulsions and collapse. In true English style, the mice got a lot of publicity and the public identified the prosecution as the villains, for their cruelty to animals. With much less furore, the accused was convicted and imprisoned for life.

One of the most horrifying aspects of the case was the evidence for the prosecution given by a doctor who talked about a visit he had made to a psychiatric hospital to observe the effects of insulin on non-diabetic patients. I knew insulin used to be used occasionally to force people with anorexia nervosa to eat; Sylvia Plath wrote a gruesome description of that in her autobiographical novel, *The Belljar*. But I had no idea it was used as a means of reducing patients' brains to malleable quagmires, presumably to make them more acquiescent to therapeutic suggestion, as this doctor so enthusiastically described. I read his report in the *Medico-Legal Journal*, which began as follows:

'Visits were made to Dr X, head of one of the largest mental hospitals in the north of England, and the actual use of insulin therapy on six women patients was watched. For nearly twenty years Dr X had used insulin therapy and had tragedies – fortunately few – in the early stages.'

I had to force myself to go on reading and to believe that the author was a human being, writing about other – and less fortunate – human beings.

'It was most dramatic to see these six women, after an overnight fast, become flushed, sweat profusely, ask for water, become languid and amenable to suggestion . . . Later, some became comatose with widely dilated fixed pupils (coma stage). Recovery was rapid after food (sopor stage) or sugar by stomach tube (coma stage) had been given. It was obvious that observation of each patient was vital for many hours after treatment, lest relapse occur. Do we know all we should about the rapidity of absorption of drugs?'

Do we know all we should about what we are doing? All I can do is pray that this so-called insulin 'therapy' has now been banished for ever, for it strikes me as morally and medically indefensible.

It is a relief to descend to the humbler levels of diabetic food manufacture – an area which I realise is of especial importance to those diabetics who can control their condition by diet alone. It is illegal to sell food claiming to be diabetic unless both its carbohydrate and calorie content are lower than those of ordinary foods and are stated as such on the label. I would not have expected the calorie requirement, although it is possibly included because many diabetic foods are made with a sweetener called sorbitol, which has more calories than sugar. I stood in a chemist's queue recently behind a fat woman who was buying a bar of diabetic chocolate made with sorbitol. She saw the label saying how many calories it had (a lot), but did not believe it because it had no sugar and she was convinced it must be less fattening than ordinary chocolate. We chatted in the queue and she finally came out with this unanswerable comment: 'Doesn't matter. Even if this sorbitol stuff is fattening, it soon comes out the other end.'

She had a point. Not a delicate one but true nevertheless. Sorbitol is made chemically from glucose and if you eat more than about two to three ounces in a day, it turns your stomach inside out. That is, I suppose, one way of losing weight, but a drastic one! Sorbitol is nasty stuff. At least, I think so. It is metabolised without insulin but it is only half as sweet as sugar, so you have to use twice as much of it to get an equivalent sweetness. It is expensive, laxative, diuretic and unappetising. It looks as if it has something to do with polystyrene. A box of it costs more than twice as much as the same amount of sugar and goes half as far.

Most diabetic chocolate, sweets and jams are made with sorbitol and don't taste too bad; not good by normal standards but pleasant enough by subnormal ones. The factory-made jams are much better than the home-made diabetic variety: I know because I have tried making jam using sugar substitute and ended up cast down by the dingy little mush of discoloured fruit I was left with. Commercially produced jam must have some chemical in it to cheer up the colour; the consistency is just right, too. As long as you limit yourself to about a teaspoonful at a time it is consoling to have something sweet to eat now and then.*

*Health food shops sell Whole Earth jams, without either sugar or artificial sweeteners. They are delicious, low calorie and can be eaten in unlimited quantities. That is the trouble. Whole Earth jam is wickedly expensive and once I have opened it I am tempted to sit with a teaspoon and a good book and read my way blissfully through a whole jar.

All diabetic jams and chocolate, in fact all diabetic foods, are more expensive than ordinary foods. I suppose that is because they are specialist products manufactured for a small market and have to be made with specialist equipment and expensive ingredients like sorbitol. Boiled sweets, fruit drops, fruit gums, fruit pastilles and sugarless chewing gum are all made with sorbitol. Saccharin is much cheaper and has a much stronger sweetening power but it is not used often in diabetic foods because it has a bitter after-taste. When you put a couple of saccharin tablets* into a cup of tea or coffee they leave a rim of greenish silt that tastes of metal. Saccharin used in sufficient quantities to make jam would make metal jam, and even sorbitol tastes a bit metallic. (Every traditional diabetic sweetener tastes like metal.) But saccharin has the twofold advantage that it contains no calories and is also relatively cheap.

Three years ago I decided to give up sweetening tablets in tea and coffee for Lent; I only took one and hoped I would soon lose the taste for sweetened drinks altogether, which many people say can happen. I should be so lucky. By the end of Lent I missed the bitter-sweet-metal taste so much that I celebrated Easter Sunday morning by having three saccharin tablets in my coffee at breakfast. I have since cut it down to two and I daresay if I tried hard I could get it down to one and maybe even do without. But I cannot be bothered.

Saccharin is at its least offensive in diabetic lemonade,

---

* Almost all the sugar-replacement sweetening tablets such as Hermesetas, Energen, Sweetex, Saxin, Shapers, Natura and Boots saccharin tablets, are made of saccharin, though a new one, Canderel, is made from aspartame, which is sweeter than sugar, and has no calories and no after-taste. However, there have been reports of potential risks to those people born with a genetic inability to metabolise phenylalinine (the amino acid present in aspartame which may cause mental retardation if allowed to build up in the brain), and this may inhibit the marketing and sale of the sweetener. Others are being developed at the moment and one can only wait and see which of them will prove useful to diabetics.

orangeade and the like. There are several makes of diabetic squash, none of them exactly lip-smacking, but none of them too bitter either; they are cloying and bland at the same time. I think Chekwate is the one I like best. Boots make their own diabetic squashes as well as a whole array of diabetic and slimming foods and drinks (the slimming ones are called Shapers). You can buy Boots diabetic chocolate, jam, marmalade, sweets, biscuits, tinned fruit, fruitcake, muesli, even honey substitute. I am waiting for the day they make diabetic lemon curd. I once wrote to Boots asking them if they were going to make diabetic white chocolate. They wrote back saying they were not sure how much of a market there would be for it but would let me know if they ever decided to reconsider. Well, I am a market, small but vigorous.

Boots diabetic products are good. They are cheaper than other makes and taste, as they say in medical bulletins, as good as can be expected. Their diabetic squashes are not great but their version of PLJ is deliciously sharp and transparent. I wrote to Boots again, asking them if I could go round one of their factories and see their diabetic foods being made. They wrote back at once and said that unfortunately it was impossible but offered to help in any other way. They also very kindly enclosed a Boots book of diets which listed all the products they make for different types of diet: sugar-free, gluten-free, reduced salt, unsaturated fat, slimming and eight other kinds of diet. Each section has an explanation of the disorder necessitating the diet, and the foods Boots make to supply them. There are pages upon pages of prices, calories and analyses of ingredients. Boots are a wonderful firm. I used to be prejudiced in favour of small shops and against supermarkets. Emotionally I still am, but not where diabetic foods are concerned.

Having stated my case for Boots, I admit that I seldom buy diabetic foods, though once in a while I buy a jar of jam and eat it half a teaspoon at a time. But the simple fact is that no diabetic food tastes as nice as food sweetened with sugar. On the whole I prefer to accept diabetes as a savoury desert and not try to alleviate it with artificial oases of sweetness, though the exception to that is the range of sugarless tinned fruit which Sainsbury's have recently brought out. I do not know whether they were inspired by the new enthusiasm for all things natural or by the ever-growing slimming market, but either way they are a welcome development. The fruit – grapefruit, pear, mandarin and pineapple – is tinned in its natural juice, without sugar added, and is delicious: far better than the sorbitol-sweetened tinned fruit that costs a pound a mouthful and floats around in metal syrup.

The one diabetic food I do have a passion for is some sweets called Vivils which come in little tubes, either lemon or peppermint flavoured. It is the lemon ones I love. They are acutely citric and only the fact that they are made with sorbitol stops me eating the whole tube straight off. Like a lot of diabetic foods, they are made in West Germany. One of the diabetic food manufacturers I wrote to asking about their products was Stute, who make good, expensive diabetic jam. They wrote back from their Bristol office saying that they could not show me round any of their factories because they are all in Germany; Bristol is just their UK distribution point. But they sent me a selection of diabetic jam labels in case I wanted to look at diabetic jam labels.

The Germans make not only diabetic jams and foods but also diabetic equipment. Most of the blood test sticks, for example, are made in Germany, which may help to explain why they are so expensive.

Maybe the Germans will come to the rescue of diabetic fizzy drinks. They are execrable. The only one that is even barely tolerable is Schweppes Slimline shandy. All the others are beyond vocabulary. To pick one at random, there is One Cal, which comes in assorted colours and flavours. It is so called because a tin of it only has one calorie. I do not think I have ever tasted anything that I have disliked so much, but then I have yet to run the whole gamut of One Cal flavours.*

However I am loath to be too rude about One Cal because it is made by Energen who were very kind to me when I wrote my standard letter asking if I could see round one of their factories. They rang me the day after I had written to them, saying they would be delighted to show me round; would I like to name a date? I had got so used to being refused that it took me a moment to take it in. The more so as Energen foods are not diabetic products; they are slimming foods which sometimes overlap with the diabetic market.

Energen is part of a large firm called RHM Foods, which has a factory in Ashford, Kent. (I love visiting factories and looked forward to going round this one.) I stayed the night with friends in London and got the breakfast train from Waterloo to Ashford. I ate some bread for breakfast at my friends' and some more on Waterloo Station, where I also had a sugary drink because I felt shaky and depressed and thought I must be going hypo. Almost every other day of the year I go hypo in the afternoon but that day I went hypo in the morning. I ate a whole packet of sweets on the train but got to Ashford at about ten o'clock still feeling awful.

The RHM factory is not far from the station and easy to find. I was met by the factory manager, Roy Drury, and the firm's research chemist and legal adviser, Brian Francis, who had come all the way down from Willesden just to show me round. Over a cup of coffee he told me the history of RHM, which I was just about switched-on enough to take in. The firm was founded in the Channel Islands in 1912 and set up in

---

*I drank some One Cal in a moment of mental aberration last summer and after one swallow read the ingredients on the label to see if they explained the horror. I think they did: carbonated water, flavourings, colour (E150), phosphoric acid, acidity regulator (sodium citrate), artificial sweetener (saccharin sodium), preservative (E211), caffeine, vitamin C. With a chemical nightmare like that, one calorie is too many.

England under the name Therapeutic Foods. I did not know people were interested in slimming foods as early as that; I had always believed that slimming foods (as distinct from plain dieting) were a modern idea. But apparently not.

Therapeutic Foods did well and after World War One moved to Bermondsey in London's Dockland, then to Willesden, where the company still has its head office, and finally to Ashford, where it has had its factory for the last thirty years. A few years ago the company was bought by J. Rank Ltd. and is now moving from the production of starch-reduced to the production of high fibre foods. That makes sense. Both diabetic and slimming diets have been putting emphasis on high fibre food in the last two or three years, and I hope that RHM do well out of this trend.

Brian Francis gave me a white cap and coat and showed me round the factory. I went all that way, caused all that trouble and all I can remember is seeing wholemeal lasagne being cut up by women in white. At one stage Brian asked me if I was all right because he said I looked pale. But I was so hypo by then that I was only semi-conscious and it was all I could do to nod my assent and carry on trailing vacantly around. I could not even ask any of the questions I wanted to ask. I do not know what they must have thought of me, but whatever it was they were too polite to pass any comment.

They took me to lunch in a pub and as soon as I had had something to eat I felt better. I apologised for myself and cursed inwardly. I could have gone back another time; I am sure they would have taken me round again, but there is a limit to the trouble and embarrassment you can bear to cause. When I left they gave me a huge package of free food: a jar of jam and one of marmalade, a packet of each of four varieties of crispbread, a box of starch-reduced rolls, a little tube of sweeteners. Luckily, I got away without any One Cal.

Energen jams and marmalade have reduced sugar levels but are not sugar-free, so I can only eat a small amount at a time.

185

Energen starch-reduced crispbreads and rolls would be more useful for non-insulin diabetics, who control their condition through diet alone and need to cut down on carbohydrate, than for people who have to eat a lot of starch, as I do.

Sweeteners and diabetic foods generally are the manageable side of diabetic control: you can take them or leave them. Work trouble, what you can and cannot do as a diabetic, crime and suspected crime, are more public – and problematic. And in between there is the mediator in the form of the BDA and the activities it organises for its members. It is the public nature of BDA activities, commendable though they are, that I dislike. I got on a train a while ago with a woman doctor who was writing out some holiday programmes for diabetics. I asked her what they were for and she said they were for a diabetic outward bound holiday camp. I am not sure I could think of anything worse. Outward bound is bad enough but diabetic outward bound would be a nightmare, as far as I am concerned. Apparently they have a good time; activities such as walking, canoeing and mountaineering are organised and medical help is always at hand. Great numbers of children seem to like diabetic holiday camps which must be a welcome respite for parents too, but I am afraid I would hate them. It is probably just a temperamental perversity, but that apart, it adds to my enjoyment of holidays to know that I am going on holiday, just like that, and not diabetically.

Diabetic holidays are part of the grey, invisible area of diabetes which only diabetics know. The public face of diabetes is made up of diabetic foods and forbidden foods on the one hand and diabetic personalities and the BDA on the other, with the horrors of insulin murders, suicides and therapy appearing every so often. But the dreary everyday prison of diabetic restraint and watchfulness remains a wasteland known only to insulin-dependent diabetics and the beast who lives there with them.

11

Body's End

Is this thy body's end?
Then, soul, live thou upon thy servant's loss . . .
(William Shakespeare, *Sonnet CXLVI*)

When I was about ten I tried not breathing to see if I could go on being alive without going through the mechanics. I held my breath until I turned purple and had spots in front of my eyes and heard a ringing in my ears. Then I started breathing again because I had to, which made me realise that I would start breathing again as soon as I became unconscious; it was automatic and it was a waste of time trying not to. Something beyond my control made me do it.

That ought to make living a matter of course, but it does not. I never get used to being alive. It remains a constant source of wonder to me. I have never been hypnotised back into the womb; I have never been dead, so I do not know what it is like to be anything except alive. Still, I can never get over it.

Often it takes me by surprise. In the middle of shopping I suddenly remember that I am not just performing a chore – I am also living. That does not make me feel different, but it does make me more aware of the essential, primitive fact of existence. I carry on shopping with a fresh sense of awe and detachment, and try to treasure that feeling even when more

187

mundane things begin to impinge: the weather, other shops I have to go to, bills I have to pay.

At other times the facts help to produce the wonder: brooding; quiet mountains; music; the sea; birds flying; trees growing; the sun; the moon; the stars; all the usual things that make people marvel at the world they live in. But the thing which makes me wonder most is the simple fact that I live in that world. Why? Why should anyone be alive? I find other people's existence almost as astonishing as my own. But not quite. Nothing is quite as intensely incomprehensible as the fact that I exist, and though I do it all the time, day in day out, night after night, I do it without trying, without even choosing. Something makes me live.

Part of what makes living so odd is death. I remember the nuns at school telling us that the only fact we know for certain once we have been born is that we are going to die. Everything else might or might not happen; death is the only certainty. In the Catholic tradition there are four last things: death, judgement, heaven and hell, of which only the first is certain. But a moment's thinking about it, which we were recommended to do every night, was enough to make me more than ever aware of being alive. To my thinking, the nuns had too long a focus: I accepted their point about death, but there was also the much more immediate and awe-inspiring fact that I was alive.

Life and death. Both natural, both inexplicable, one of them surprising. But I would find it even more surprising if the reason for life *were* understandable. I ask myself why I am alive, but not seriously; I would not seriously expect to know. Any more than I would expect to know why I am like I am: why I have brown hair and freckles, why I hate chemistry, why I like apples and champagne, why I am diabetic.

I have never asked myself that last question. If I am diabetic because God wants it, it would be a waste of time to ask why. I would be less inclined to worship a God I could understand; the next step would be giving Him advice. If there is no God, there is no one to ask why I am diabetic anyway. So I don't.

And if I did ask why, it would not be why have I got diabetes but why have I *only* got diabetes? Why have I not got cancer? Why am I not blind or deaf, or suffering any of the terrible diseases that other people endure? Why was I born into a home where I had love and enough to eat?

Given that the sheer fact of life itself is so amazing, any good things about it are a bonus over and above this absolute and in that sense harder to understand than the misery life also contains. The only time I can remember asking why about something painful was in India. Before going there I was so used to accepting life as it came that I panicked when I found myself asking why things had to be agonising. One day I was walking back to my hostel when I saw a man lying on the pavement in front of me. The massed crowds that pour down every Indian street parted on either side of him like the sea round a rock and he lay ignored, whimpering. When I stooped down to see if there was anything I could do to help, I saw that his feet were mostly rotted away. He was a leper and his face, which was patched with white blotches, was beginning to rot too, and one side of his mouth was eaten away deep into his cheek with purplish suppurations around the wound.

There was nothing I could do to help. I did not speak his language. He whimpered and I just looked at him and put my hand on his filthy, oily head. Some of the people pouring past looked at me fleetingly, and accusingly. For all I knew I might have been insulting him or breaking some caste or religious custom by touching him. I must have looked patronising. So I stood up and went home, the question 'why?' exploding inside my head. I told one of the sisters about him and asked her how she managed to get used to the

189

poverty and illness she saw around her. She said she had never got used to it, even after working in India for thirty years. I then asked her if she had ever questioned why things were like that. 'All the time,' she replied, and added with a sad smile, 'I haven't got an answer yet. I try to see the good things as well as the bad. It's hard but it's the only way to get by.'

I tried to do that too, but I had run out of time. Everything I saw made me miserable. When eventually I calmed down it was not because I had found an answer but because I accepted that there probably was a reason for everything which I neither could, nor should, know. All I could do with painful problems was fight them and try to accept them at the same time.

It is hard to get the right balance between fighting and accepting. I do not count my diabetes as being anywhere near as serious as the suffering I saw in India, and I know that people suffer everywhere. It is small beer. But the principles of handling it are the same. By fighting, I mean defying the beast and, more prosaically, sticking to the rules. The only way I can fight diabetes psychologically is to go on as if I had not got it, though I know I have; to act as if I were free, though I know the beast is closer to me than my own breathing.

By accepting diabetes I mean keeping to the diets they give me, injecting the insulin they tell me to inject, rotating injection sites, and making sure I balance exercise with extra starch when necessary. That is the only way to make light of my condition and as it comes over pretty heavy a lot of the time anyway, I fight it hard.

But there is another way of fighting diabetes; a more concealed way. When I was first diagnosed, and began to realise what diabetes could mean in my life, I asked myself what I had been given this for; what possible good could I get out of it? Maybe I could get willpower, which would be forced on me by having to keep to injections, diet and so on; I could develop more sympathy and patience with people; maybe I could even get courage, which I had never needed urgently before.

This last answer embarrassed me. I thought it was over-stating the situation and so I decided to concentrate on willpower and try to build on the little I already had. I probably would have decided that, even if I had not believed in God and been brought up to 'make something of' suffering; you might as well take any affliction for what it has got.

With a stronger will I could do more, perhaps even *be* more. That was the theory. In fact I have not managed to increase my willpower at all. If anything, I have weakened it. I only keep to the rules because I have to. It is as simple, and as pathetic, as that.

I still have periodic drives for greater willpower and would still like to better it, as most people would, but I have humbler expectations now. Even if I were to become a shining paragon of determination, I am more sceptical now about how much difference that would make to my life. Inwardly, perhaps, but outwardly – I am dubious. It's prob-ably sour grapes, but even when I was about fourteen and full of romantic notions, I did not believe what some of the girls at school held to be true: namely, that you could get anything you really wanted in life if only you wanted it enough. We did not know much either about life or wanting then. And though I did not know any more than the rest of them, it struck me as obvious that you did not always get what you wanted, even if you wanted it with all the power of your being. Against huge unknowns like illness, poverty and love, such romantic notions would not stand a chance. It might be romantic to overcome impossible obstacles but it was closer to the truth for them to overcome you and for you to be brave and inwardly invincible about it.

But where illness is concerned, I was right about not

191

having a chance against it and wrong about that being romantic. I do not believe that you can overcome illness by sheer spiritual or mental willpower. The close relationship between the two works both ways: matter can get on top of mind as much as vice versa. You can do plenty to fight an illness or a condition, plenty towards getting over it, plenty to stop it spoiling your life. But you cannot ultimately *overcome* it. Maybe it is possible to overcome psychosomatic illnesses, but not a condition like diabetes.

Others would disagree with that tenet. The many disciples of 'fringe' medicine believe that all illnesses have a psychosomatic or spiritual dimension to them, but I do not. Holistic medicine, for example, aims at the positive promotion of good health by treating the whole person, unlike conventional medicine which corrects specific afflictions.

But this 'whole person' philosophy bothers me. If it means each individual complete with temperament, moods, lifestyle and so forth, of course I accept that it is the whole person who must be treated. And often in diabetic conventional medicine it is. Diabetologists are keen on taking things like temperament into account and adjusting treatment in relation to them. But I have a feeling that the holistic 'whole person' is more than that; it is held to be the spirit in ultimate control of the body, including the part of the body that is afflicted. That is why it bothers me. I went to supper recently with two converts to a branch of holistic medicine, called chiropractice, which seems to be a kind of supernatural massage, acupuncture and herbal medicine cure, with an emphasis on the training of the mind towards health. I was interested in what they told me, but remained unconvinced. I am predisposed to be receptive to any approach or technique that might help one to be healthy. But I am still sceptical about the implication that underpinned everything they said – namely, that mind and spirit are the sole controlling agents in health.

One of them claimed that his body threw up symptoms of illness whenever he wanted to escape from life. With the help of a holistic doctor he was now able to stop himself doing that and considered himself well enough to face anything. The other told me how he had spent years being treated for tension by doctors and psychiatrists who stuffed him full of pills until the day he turned round and told himself it was all wrong. He was healthy: all he needed to do was get rid of the mental block that had caused his tension, whatever that was, and he would be cured. He gave up conventional medicine and with the help of a holistic doctor is now a hundred per cent well. I am prepared to believe his particular claim. But somehow I cannot believe that he would feel fighting fit if he had a brain tumour and treated that with nothing but positive thinking.

This cynicism apart, I am nevertheless sure that it helps to have a positive attitude; in fact I know it does. I also agree that two people with the same complaint can fare quite differently. But in the end all the positive thinking in the world cannot remove a tumour. Nor can it make me produce my own insulin again. I do not think my diabetes is the result of a mental block; I wish I did, because then I might be able to get rid of it. But I cannot.

When I began work on this chapter I decided to ask an acupuncture clinic in Oxford to put me in touch with someone who had experience in this area of alternative medicine, as I did not want to write anything unfairly sceptical. I subsequently spent a whole afternoon with a young diabetic woman who said she felt much better since having acupuncture treatment. She had sacrificed her time to talk to me and come across as being refreshingly down-to-earth and clearheaded. She took care to explain that she still takes insulin and still attends clinics at the hospital, but would not feel nearly as well without her additional acupuncture therapy.

I found what she said provocative, but in the end unconvincing. I could not pin her down as to exactly what her newly-found well-being comprised; she said her blood sugar still varied to make her hypo and hyper but all the same she felt better in a way she could not define. I suppose she meant she felt more relaxed, more equable, less frightened. That I can understand and value. But after two hours of talking I could not believe that there was any concrete improvement as a result of acupuncture. She was tolerant of my scepticism, saying that the doctors at the hospital shared it; if she told them she felt better they said it must be because her blood sugar control had improved. She thought they were blind to the 'whole person', just as I thought that acupuncturists, judging from the book about acupuncture she lent me, were blind to the flesh and blood person, scientifically understood.

I do not know. I am probably blinded by Western science, but I still think there is such a thing as pure physical illness. If any one of the many branches of holistic medicine could systematically cure physical illness, then I might believe in it. But as it is, my belief is limited. If mind over matter were possible, there would be less illness and presumably, pushing it to its logical extremes, less death. But I cannot believe this is possible, not completely; not in any culture, ethos or religion.

When I was teaching at Cheltenham Ladies College I became friendly with a Christian Scientist who taught drama there. I stayed with her for a few days one summer and she told me about the Christian Scientist view of medicine which, as I understood it, preaches that illness is caused by sin and can therefore be overcome by spiritual strength. Medicines, pills and drugs are unacceptable because they are expressions of a reductionist, secular view that illness is the result of physical causes.

She told me that she had once contracted a severe bout of

malaria when she was out in the Far East but had refused quinine. She lay in the heat, sweating and shivering, and after each period of unconsciousness insisted that they were not to give her any medicine under any circumstances. She was ill for a long time then got better. In cases of malaria, I did not know how common a recovery like that without the benefit of drugs was, but I thought her experience certainly very impressive.

Her explanation struck me as being less so. I asked her how she had mastered her illness and she said that she had focused on ideal goodness and willed herself towards it. In that way she had been able to transcend evil, including her illness. I did not know what she meant and was unhappy about thinking of illness as an evil. I suppose the best – and only – way to think of ideal goodness is in human form, which for a Christian means Christ. But to concentrate on Christ so totally that you overcome illness would be almost impossible for someone as distractable and doubtful as me. She would say that is because I am lacking in faith and that she only did what the sick people in the Bible did: kept going towards Jesus until He healed them. I can see her point but it seems a narrowing one; a narrow view of illness *per se*, and a narrow view of both God and humanity in relation to illness.

I daresay that illness is bound up with the imperfect nature of life, which in turn is bound up with the existence of evil, but not simply. I certainly do not believe that anyone's suffering through illness is a punishment for being evil. It is not in my interests to believe that. Nor do I believe that being ill is falling under the power of evil; it is a fact of life and life is often cryptic about its good and evil – and how they are apportioned. Illness is horrible but that does not mean it is bad. What about all those inspiring examples of people becoming heroes and saints because of their afflictions, finding strength they did not have before? Their sufferings might have been appalling but what they achieved *through* them was not. I know it is flying in the face of my Christian Scientist friend's experience but I do not believe that being good or holy in itself has any actual effect on health. Believing in God has no effect on it either. Nor does wanting to be well, except in areas where willpower obviously makes a difference, such as in the will to overcome psychosomatic illness and in the endurance of unpleasant treatment like radiotherapy for cancer. I am open-minded but sceptical about faith healing.

I am what the Christian Scientists would call a reductionist about illness, insofar as I believe that only doctors and medicines have a direct effect. Indirect effects can be produced by willpower, up to a point, and temperament, again up to a point. I can offer no other explanation for my friend's recovery, except good luck and her sheer determination to live.

I am not excluding God from the picture. It is just that I consider it is doing Him a disservice to think of Him mechanically; to think that if you ask God to make you better He will. Sometimes He does. One of the most forceful aspects of the gospels is their sympathy; instead of striking people down when they made trouble, as so often happened in the Old Testament, Jesus healed people. But only as a sign of His utterly incomprehensible, unimaginable nature. Jesus may have performed such miracles because He wanted to help people who were ill but the main reason was to make them believe, witness the paralytic let down through the roof; and to reward belief, witness the woman with the haemorrhages who followed Him until she could touch the hem of His garment. The point of miracles performed on request and prayers answered on request is belief in God; they are more of a means than an end, and they are rare.

I do not think 'Ask and you shall receive' means 'Ask and you shall receive what you want.' That would be like Huckleberry Finn, who decided he would believe in God if God helped him catch fish. He prayed to God for a fishing line and, to his amazement, found one by the river. He tried several times for the hooks but had no luck, so he gave up on God.

I have a bit of a blind spot over that sort of literal approach and hardly ever use it; it is one approach but not, to me, a very trusting one. Usually when I ask God for something specific I am not aware of receiving anything and have to trust that He knows what I want and, of course, what He has given me. I am indefinite about praying. I pray all the time, on and off, in one way or another, though I can count on the fingers of one hand the number of times I have prayed for something definite. I do not like deep and mysterious answers to prayer, but those are the answers I usually get. Those few times when I have received something specific, it has almost always been the last thing I wanted.

I admire people who are humble enough to ask for what they want and to go on asking even though they are disappointed time and again. I have never prayed to get better. It is not because I am frightened of not getting better; that would leave me no worse off than I am now. It is because I have this feeling that God knows how much I hate my diabetes and knows why I have got it, though I do pray for help in living with it. I neither expect nor get clear answers to that but I am sure I get something, though I don't know what it is; maybe acceptance, maybe courage. I just don't know.

It is impossible to weigh a condition against a quality but, if pushed, I would say that over the years diabetes has given me more than it has taken away. It has given me a measure of sympathy, patience, and understanding; a rather frantic appreciation of feeling well and possibly a sort of strength. It is not the noble sort, though. It is grim strength – I last things out with grim persistence, which is not the most dashing of acquisitions.

On the debit side, I have lost my carelessness and, though I hate to say it, my easy enjoyment of life. I still enjoy life but not as effortlessly as I used to. And sometimes I also now detest it. Obviously that is partly because I am older and life cannot go on being a sunny summer afternoon, but I know that it is also because I am shadowed by the beast.

God, how I hate the beast. It is the worst thing in my life, the only thing that is worse than actually feeling hypo. I live like a wren in a hurricane, struggling against the dread of approaching hypos. I hate that so much that even if diabetes had given me countless virtues – some unique insight even – I would still rather be without it.

When I go hypo I get miserable; not always visibly but inside myself. I cannot help it. Misery is a prime constituent of hypoglycaemia. Afterwards I am just happy to be feeling well again, but at the time there is nothing to feel except abject misery. I surprised myself in the winter of 1982 when I had an appalling hypo which plunged me into despair and took me – or at least I thought it took me – to the point where all I had to do was give up and I would die.

I was taking long-acting insulin and woke up in the early morning paralysed but able to move enough to drop out of bed and work my way across the floor and along the landing to the top of the stairs, where I stopped because I could not go on. I had bought a new packet of Dextrose that day but had forgotten – the only time I have ever forgotten – to put it beside my bed. I had to get downstairs and into the kitchen but could not think how to do it. Besides feeling ill and shivery, I felt queasy and dizzy, which I had never felt in a hypo before. I lay with my head hanging down over the top stair and the ceiling began to slide around above me. Spots popped up in front of my eyes and I knew that I would lose consciousness any minute.

I managed to roll over on to my front and hang my arms down on to the third or fourth stair, intending to crawl down. At least I think that is what I intended. But whatever it was, I was too hypo to do it. I put my weight on my hands and my arms buckled, my head hit the step and I fell downstairs. The stairs have a right-angle bend two-thirds of the way down and I rocketed into it, then crashed straight down on to the floor without touching the last few steps. I hit my head so hard that I blacked out, and when I came round everything hurt. I had never hurt so much. My ribs felt like stabbing knives whenever I drew breath. I started to cry but it hurt so much down my side that I stopped and lay still, trying to will myself to move.

The carpet sloped away under me and the ceiling became a sliding mass of spots and pain. I counted to ten then turned over on to my front, but it hurt so much that I screamed; not loudly because I did not have the strength, just weakly. I started to drag myself across the floor, a few inches at a time, trying to think what it would be like when I got to the kitchen and found some sugar. When, not if.

Finally, I reached the kitchen, feeling the lino cold beneath me. My neck and head stabbed so much that I longed to take them off and put them somewhere else. But once I was in the kitchen I felt a spasm of hope. All I had to do was get some sugar. But I could not. It was up on the shelf and I was down on the floor. I pulled myself along to the far end of the kitchen, where I knew the sugar was stored, and collapsed on to my back.

There was deep snow outside. It shone white through the French doors and made the kitchen light, and bitterly cold. My feet had gone numb and I could not have balanced on them even if I could have got myself upright. I sweated icily. Black patches came and went over my eyes. In between them I saw the flex of the coffee percolator hanging down from the shelf. The sugar was somewhere near the coffee: if I could pull the coffee down I might be able to bring the sugar with it. I stretched up my hand, which waved about as if it did not belong to me, and all at once caught the lead. The coffee and sugar crashed down all over me.

I can never get over how much more there is of anything when it is loose than when it is contained: the minute the coffee and sugar were spilt, they assumed prodigious proportions. Coffee granules splattered all across the floor, the wall, the fridge, the door and, most depressingly, my face. Cold coffee dripped out of my hair. The sugar bowl had cracked when it hit the floor and lay next to the percolator in two pieces, coffee seeping over the sugar and turning it brown. There were brown splashes on my nightie and in the bright light I could see that my legs were bruised red, purple and blue.

I licked sugar and cold coffee off the floor, then lay and waited to feel better. But I was violently sick and immediately felt so ill that it came to me suddenly that I might die. I was probably wrong. I would probably have gone into a coma and come out of it later. But I had a feeling I was going to die then and there. I had lost the little bit of sugar I had swallowed and was more hypo than I ever remembered feeling while still conscious. Sweat, sugar and coffee poured off my face and hair. My legs were numb and shaking. I could not see properly; everything was blurred and blotched with black. I did not have an ounce of strength left. I knew I could lose consciousness if I wanted; all I had to do was lay my head on the floor. But it was more than that; I had a feeling that if I did that, if I gave in to it, I would not wake up. I could simply close my eyes and be released from the nightmare I was caught in.

A prayer flashed across my mind; not a coherent one but a desperate plea not to be taken to a place where the nightmare would go on and on, where the beast would be with me forever and I would be in hell. Whether it was that thought that did it, I do not know – it came and went in a split second – but I knew without consciously thinking about it that I had to stay alive. It was not a choice. It was a compulsion. I found myself licking up sugar like a mad thing. I swallowed it and was sick again. The more sugar I swallowed, the more sick I was and the more sick I was, the more hypo. I had no resources left within me, except the sheer fact of wanting to live.

Luckily, I never locked the kitchen door and was able to open it by waving my hand above my head until I hit the handle. The freezing cold blew in. I pushed one half of the sugar bowl along the floor with my face, trailing the ends of my hair through the vomit. I lifted the half bowl over the doorstep with my teeth and dropped it in the snow, shoved my face in after it and swallowed mouthfuls of snow full of sugar. I do not know why I did it. Nor do I know why, or how, I was not sick again but I was not. I licked the bowl clean and for the first time since I had woken up, the spots and patches cleared from my sight. I could clearly see the half bowl lying in the snow.

The other half of the bowl was in the middle of the floor and I licked the sugar out of it, feeling grotesquely sick but managing not to be. I felt a bit better and stopped shaking so uncontrollably. I opened the door of the fridge and got out a carton of orange juice which I drank without spilling more than half of it. My nightie was a collage of orange, coffee, vomit and sugar.

As soon as you are out of hypos they shrink to their actual size. The time-scale returns to normal: the horrors are only memories. I sat on the floor surrounded by the effluent of my hypo and realised that it had not lasted more than ten minutes from beginning to end. Relief overwhelmed me: I was alive again. I started cleaning up and switched my self-pity to my aches and pains.

I decided that I must have been wrong about being at death's door; it must have been a distortion, like everything else to do with hypos. But even if it was a distortion, from inside the hypo it was true. I only survived because something made me survive. I have always thought that it is inadequate to say that life is a gift; now I know it for certain. It is a gift certainly, like death; either that or it has no first cause, which I cannot believe. But it is not just a gift. It is not just given to me. It *is* me. It is not an extra or a possession; it is my essence and I have no choice about it. If I had had a choice, I would have let it go, but all I had was a life force I could not resist.

12

Its Crest and its Showers

King of the Tree of Life, with its flowers,
The space around which noble hosts were ranged,
Its crest and its showers on every side spread
Over the fields and plains of Heaven.
(Author Unknown, Irish, AD 988)

I do not think suffering is good for you. I never have thought that and I never will. I think it can be, if you take it right, but that is all. If I could, I would get rid of my diabetes faster than the speed of light. I think it is a perversion of Christianity to want suffering. I heard a woman talking about the Carmelite religious order and she said that one of their favourite mottos was 'A day without suffering is a day wasted.' That, to me, is a kind of madness. A day without suffering is a day to be grateful for. St John of the Cross, who was a great friend of the Carmelites, said that you should try to have your purgatory here on earth. He would. But I would not. I would like a good time here on earth and then to be saved by mercy – or last-minute repentance.

Life is what you can get away with. Michael used to go round endlessly reciting a couplet written in honour of Oscar Wilde by an Irish folk poet.

'Tis sweet, the life of a sinner; sweet to die with God's praise,
My life on you, Oscar boy; yourself had it both ways.

203

Quite. That's the ideal. While I never pray to get better I never pray to get worse either. I am too English to do that, and too attracted to having it both ways. Other people are more selfless. The Spaniards have a terrifying leaning towards the fanatical. There is a story of a Spanish saint who prayed to be given other people's illnesses. If she did it to spare them, I love her for it. If she did it to improve her character, she was plainly off her head. Either way, she was given illness after illness and in the end could not stand it any more and broke down, begging God to restore her to health. She was lucky; He did.

From the little I know about it, I would say that people who are afflicted with suffering and take it bravely do as much good to the people around them as they do to themselves. Perhaps even more. I only work at St Joseph's Hospice one week in the year now but the first time I went I stayed several months; each time I go back I come away feeling stronger and revitalised. It is a sad place, full of death, but it is not depressing because at the same time it is imbued with hope.

The hospice has two wings: one for people who are expected to die quickly, within days or, at most, weeks, and the other for people who have long-term illnesses and cannot look after themselves anymore. I have worked in both and do not know which is the more harrowing.

Watching people die is fearful. I am not at all resigned and religious about it. All I can take in is that someone has died; they were there just a minute, a second ago, and now they are gone and nothing can bring them back. That is the only reality; anything else is just a hope or a belief.

Watching people living in the long-stay wing is fearful in a different way. It is less obliterating but more insidious. Some of the patients have been there for years, like John, a merchant seaman with a broken back who cannot move and has no one to take care of him. I hate to see the people there, whom I have got to know a little over the years, that much weaker each time. I hate to see them humiliated by being incontinent or unable to speak or eat. And, most harrowing of all, I hate to see them in pain. The first time I heard someone shrieking in agony in St Joseph's I went on hearing it for weeks afterwards. There are no words to describe what it was like.

But in all the years I have worked at the hospice I have never heard anyone ask to be killed. I have heard people say that they want to die; but that is different from wanting to be killed. I am always humbled by the courage of patients like John, who is in constant pain but hardly ever complains. When he feels very low I have heard him say that he wishes it was all over, but later he hangs on again, quietly and magnificently.

In 1982 I worked as a domestic in the short-stay wing where I remember one patient in particular. This man had tubes coming out of his nose and throat and lay all day doing nothing. He could not eat and had to be fed through his tubes. The smell around his bed was rank, and he was deathly pale and thin. I do not know what was wrong with him, but he was an inspiration. He smiled whenever I took him a clean jug of water or cleaned his bedside table, though neither of these were any use to him. He stayed awake while the others slept after lunch and I used to look up and find him smiling at me. When I left they told me he would not live more than another day, but in the week I was there he lifted my heart.

I knew nothing about that man; I did not even know his name. I do not know whether his illness had made him serene and uncomplaining or whether that was in his nature anyway. But whichever it was, the way in which he died had a strong effect on everyone there. I was reminded of the only poem Gerard Manley Hopkins wrote when he was in Liverpool, about a dying man, a blacksmith called Felix

Randal. Hopkins describes what it was like to watch him 'pining, pining' beneath his illness. Then there was a change:

Sickness broke him. Impatient, he cursed at first, but mended . . .
This seeing the sick endears them to us, us too it endears.
My tongue had taught thee comfort, touch had quenched thy tears,
Thy tears that touched my heart, child, Felix, poor Felix Randal . . .

Hopkins is so right. Seeing the sick endears them to us. The man I saw dying in St Joseph's was officially useless but unofficially wonderful. And Hopkins is right about comfort too. The illness does not have to be fatal and the comforter does not have to be a friend; anyone's comforting of any sick person is invaluable.

It is really impossible to describe how much difference even one word of sympathy makes. I try to think of that when I get annoyed with people; when I am elbowed out of the way in a queue or have my bike lights pinched. Whoever is responsible may be feeling ill; they may be hypo or depressed or on the verge of suicide, and my reaction could tip the balance. Just hearing someone say 'All right, luv?' when I am staggering around knocking their shopping all over the road can lift my spirits and keep me in the world I am losing touch with.

In a way comforting friends is easier than comforting strangers: you help friends naturally and it deepens the friendship. But the trouble with me is, it is always my turn to be helped. Where health is concerned, I ask so much more of my friends than they ask of me, and my health always seems to be concerned, even when it has no right to be – to the extent that I give close friends part of the beast to carry around. James asks me how I am all the time; he force-feeds me with biscuits when there is no need just in case. That is shouldering the beast and it lifts a dead weight. When I am with friends like James I feel safe; enough to breathe a bit freely and – more precious still – live a bit carelessly.

If I had to pick a word to describe what I feel like most of the time it would be tired. The little time I spend in the middle ground between hypo and hyper I spend feeling drained. And it is not normal, welcome tiredness – the sort you feel after a hard day's work – it is a different kind altogether, a hybrid of the draining exhaustion of hyperglycaemia and the destructive weariness of the beast. I do not reckon it worth thinking about. I have only tried to define it for the purpose of writing this book, and I wish I had not. The tiredness I am talking about is feeling tired of living. In spirit I do not feel that at all and I definitely do not feel tired of life – but the fact remains that it always feels like three o'clock in the afternoon in my life. The tide is always out and there is a long way to walk.

Fighting that is easy, but hard work all the same. Being aware of tiredness makes you feel more weary still. I was brought up with a fresh air, no nonsense attitude to things like tiredness and I still have it, but nowadays it is tempered. I admit to tiredness as a positive condition. It is not an important one but it is a classic example of the sort of nagging aggravation one is morally bound to ignore in order to be 'above it all'. I ignore it because it is there and has to be ignored, if it is not to get stronger. Even when I want to cry tears of exhaustion and long to fall into bed, I ignore it and force myself to carry on.

If diabetes is a second division complaint, then tiredness is most definitely a third, which makes them both an indulgence to write about and a burden to live with. I am so cross with myself on the rare occasions when I let myself seem as depleted as I feel, that I try to be exceptionally sympathetic to other people who suffer in the same way. And I know that there are people whose lives leave them feeling cruelly tired. Telling people how tired I am is tedious. I prefer to think wistfully of the psalm, 'Their life will be like a watered garden; they will never be weary again.'

I have come to the conclusion that everything about health is boring except the fact of health itself. Whereas I have always thought of life as a continuing miracle I have only realised since being diabetic that health is too. It is not the norm from which illness is a decline; it is an ineffable extra. I once saw a medical student on television arguing that there was no such thing as good or bad health; what was health for one person might be illness for the next. But to me that is a romantic idea of illness which only someone who has never felt seriously ill could hold. He is right to believe that health is not a norm but that is surely because it is a benediction, not because it is negotiable.

Health is different from not being ill. I cannot define the difference but I can feel it. I often feel quite well but I have not felt absolutely well for twelve years. One day, maybe, I will completely forget what it is like to feel perfectly well, and the more negative 'not feeling ill' will take its place as the optimum. But so far I have not forgotten. On the contrary, I can do more than remember; I can picture it in my mind's eye; see what it felt like inside my body, blazing with health. I have a glorified idea of health and look upon it as something brilliant, as surprising and gratuitous as life and as exciting as safety, which frees you for anything.

When I have good days and feel reasonably well, I burn them up. I do not necessarily do a great deal but I bask in being able to do it. I do not look around, in case I see the beast. I do not acknowledge that I feel tired, in case it deflates me. Instead, I remind myself every half hour that I feel well, in case I start taking it for granted. Perhaps if I felt well all the time, as I used to, I would become blasé, like I used to be, and not appreciate health as an abundance above and beyond being alive. But I would be willing to take that risk, for I have not forgotten the treasure of feeling nothing but well. I could never forget what that is like any more than I could ever forget the beast and all its dingy relatives: tiredness, apprehension, resignation, fear and depression.

I live with them all; the whole beastly family has moved in with me, except depression, thank God. That must be the worst. I get depressed when I am hypo but that is literally and physically; my spirit is pushed down, along with my blood sugar, to below living level. The lower the blood sugar, the more intense the depression. And the degrees of depression during a hypo are many: the bottom one, where you are not alive; the one where you know you are alive but know that it would be better not to be; the one where you are well enough to fight but know you cannot win; the one where you are desperately miserable and need help; and the top one, where you are depressed and miserable but still able to envisage safety on the other side of the margin.

In fact the depression most diabetics feel after a hypo (and which I am lucky enough not to feel, except later in a generalised way, as an awareness of the beast) is nothing like the depression you feel during one. It is altogether different; bearable and tinged with relief. Apart from hypos, which are a world of their own, I do not think diabetes has depressed me. It has certainly shadowed my life but that makes me fight all the harder and revel in the times when I do feel better. I cannot see any point in getting depressed about diabetes. It would be a life sentence – a vicious circle of illness and diabetic depression – and make the condition more burdensome.

Perhaps I have not had it long enough. I know now that it gets worse as the years progress, and that I shall probably develop all sorts of complications. But that does not depress me either. Sometimes, not believing in the future can be a blessing.

Too much thinking about one's life is a menace, and too much worrying about the state of one's health is fatal. It is like happiness; as soon as you start thinking about it, you have lost it. But then, more maddening still, as soon as you have lost it, you know you were happy and damn yourself for not enjoying it more when the going was good.

Thinking about it intellectually, which I never usually do, is even more subversive. Standards of comparison creep up higher, so your condition in relation to them goes down. Everyone else looks better off than you. The handicap of diabetes is a bit like Parkinson's law: it expands to fill the space allotted to it, and psychologically that is disastrous.

Because you are never free of diabetes, not for a single minute, you cannot get close enough to what the healthy past was like, or indeed to what a healthy future might be like, to feel that you are within reach of either. There is no hope, so there can be no disappointment. If diabetes were curable; if one in a thousand diabetics could get free of it, it would be much more unnerving – and unbearable. If it came and went, like migraine, it would then engender false hopes that there might never be a next time. But there always is: diabetes is permanent and constant. Even if it is stable, with very few ups and downs, you still have to do the injections each day. They become habitual, part of life's routine like cleaning your teeth, but I know that if I had just one day without having to inject myself, I would scarcely be able to make myself go back to the diabetic norm. It would be a taste of the forbidden fruit, and as such irresistible.

So far, though, I *have* managed to resist. I need three injections a day and have not tried skipping them because it would be too wonderful and I would feel too ill. But it happens to people and I can imagine it happening to me only too vividly. You suddenly reach a point where you just cannot do another injection. Something snaps inside you.

A man I once saw at the Radcliffe Infirmary was a case in point. He was twenty-eight and had been diabetic since he was six months old. I do not know how many injections he had per day, probably one or two, but however many it was he suddenly could not do another. He knew he would die without injections. He had had injections and then injected himself without any trouble for twenty-eight years but one morning he got up, looked at the syringe in the bathroom and could not make himself use it.

The doctors tried to talk him out of it but nothing they said made any difference. I went past the ward on my way to have a bath and saw him lying in bed, crying, with huge, shuddering sobs. I heard him saying, 'All I want is a holiday from diabetes; just a few days of my life without it; just a few days without having to stick one of those bloody things into me.'

It was horrible. I lay in the bath and did not want to come out, in case he was still crying. I stayed in the bath so long, topping up the hot water, that the nurse came and asked if I was all right. He was quiet when I went past his ward, and looked as if he was asleep. I had to go back a week later and he had gone. Perhaps he had pulled himself out of the phobia. Perhaps not. But I will never forget the way he cried.

I know I could become like that as easily as falling off a knife-edge. Although I am perfectly calm and automatic about injections, I only have to close my eyes and think about a day without them to make myself feel light-headed. I must have done nearly ten thousand injections in the last twelve years, and I know I cannot do without them. But if the day ever dawns when someone finds a way to take insulin without injections, they will hear me singing a mile away.

I dread to think what effect all this injecting and beast-watching has had on my personality. James once said he thought it had made me a perfectionist, especially about people. But I doubt if that is because of diabetes; I was always like that. In fact I think I am less like that now than I used to be. Before I was diabetic, I knew everything was possible. I was only interested in the top and bottom layers of life; the middle could stay tepid and untouched. I liked people who were high fliers. I still do. At heart I am still unrealistic about people and about life, but in practice I am much milder now and more tolerant. The middle ground looks harder to hang on to and I respect people who manage to do it.

I used to be an unstoppable optimist but not any more, except in an ultimate, mysterious sense. That is one of the things that has changed most about me. People regard me as very optimistic and I am certainly not pessimistic, but I am a drizzle compared with my former, non-diabetic self. I can no longer find it in me to hope for the best. That would be ruinous. I hope a lot; hope is my weakest virtue now and I work hard at it; but it is a radically inhibited hope, a heavily qualified hope. Diabetes is only one of a galaxy of things that have happened to me since I was twenty-one to make me weaker on hope and stronger on faith, but I suspect that if I talked to a psychiatrist and poured out everything, diabetes would figure larger than I think. Whatever pluses it has given me, diabetes remains intransigent as a blight on possibility.

Michael knew me before and after my diabetes appeared on the scene and thought it was a calamity though, like all calamities, one which should not be taken seriously. He was never as optimistic as I once had been, thinking instead that good and bad things were equally unimportant. He did not give a damn about time and place; he did not care about wealth or poverty; he did not attach importance to events. Life seemed unreal to him: things happened but they were always beside the point, which was metaphysical.

I never agreed with that. I remember having an argument with Michael about whether everything mattered, which is

212

what I thought, or nothing mattered, which is what he thought, whereupon he got so heated about it that he drove straight into a roundabout and wedged the car half-way into its flowerbed. While we waited for a gap in the traffic so we could back out, with me pushing the bonnet for all I was worth, and spoiling my only good pair of shoes in the mud, he waved his arm at the tulips surrounding us and the honking cars behind and said, 'You see how much it doesn't matter.'

I did. But I thought my shoes mattered in a small way, and I thought it would have mattered if we had hit another car. Life has always seemed real to me; only too real. I have never had that sense of things being a delusion which is common to other-worldly religious people like Michael. I am a this-worldly religious person, impregnated with the reality of life. But I have moved closer to Michael's brand of optimism; a kind of nihilistic hope that something will happen, whether good or bad.

Michael was a great fan of Mr Micawber, whereas my father considers him to be the archetypal feckless, irrespon-sible waster. When Michael first announced that Mr Micawber was his ideal, my father countered flatly that it was unfair to everyone to wait for something to turn up because things seldom did. Michael swelled up like a toad because – for once – facts were on his side. Something had turned up for Mr Micawber in the end; he had gone to Australia and made his fortune.

I am less of an optimist and more of a Micawber these days; a longer-shot optimist, I suppose. I hope softly and loosely in the back of my mind that something will turn up. But unlike Michael, I would prefer it to be something good. I value happiness higher than anything else in life, except holiness, which is on a different plane and does not bear comparison. I have a huge capacity to be happy and despite the diabetes, despite the beast, I quite often am.

That is a lot to be able to say. I am lucky. For ultimately, diabetes has not made me sad. In a way, Michael and I were both right; everything matters and nothing matters, and that applies to diabetes too. It matters. I would be a fool to say it did not; I would be a fool to think I will ever feel really well again, or to hope for it. But it does not matter.

Here I am sitting at a desk with a pen in my hand, my body covered with needle marks and bruises, my blood full of sugar, my toes numb, my fingertips white. I feel tired and heavy. There are flowers on the desk in front of me and there is the beast behind me. I am diabetic and I am sitting here trying to work out what difference that makes. I will never know, and would never really want to know. Diabetes has not stopped me being blessed with life. Of that I feel certain.

All I have done is write down some facts; the truth is out of my depth, beyond my reach. And I like that. I welcome it. It takes the diabetes out of its depth, too, to where it is helpless. The beast is only a beast after all, and as long as the waters are too deep for me to stand up in, the beast will drown. And as long as I believe in God, I will be out of my depth.

Publisher's Note

Teresa McLean wrote *Metal Jam* over a period of six months, and completed the typescript in the spring of 1984. Shortly afterwards Teresa married and moved to Cambridge where she now lives with her husband, a history don.

At the end of January 1985 Teresa gave birth to a son, christened Peter.

Index

Main references are in **bold**. Page numbers followed by *n* refer to footnotes.

218

220

221

223